HOSHAW

THE AMISH
A Pioneer Heritage

Text, Photos & Design
by John M. Zielinski

Acknowledgement: I would like to thank all those Amish who have patiently borne my probing eye over the last 12 years and all those of Amish descent who have helped me in my researches into earlier pioneers. My especial and posthumous thanks to Prof. Melvin Gingerich who was to have done the introduction to this book and gave me invaluable aid in the form of research material. I only wish that he might have lived to see the job done. I hope that it lives up to his expectations.

I would also like to thank Jack and Jean Ervin of the Adams Press for permission to reprint a number of my photographs from Portrait of Iowa which they published in 1974.

Special thanks to Sylvester R. Miller, Editor, The Budget, Sugar Creek, Ohio, and all his correspondents for permission to use material from that paper.

Library of Congress Catalog Card Number 75-21328
ISBN: 0-87069-125-2

Photography by
John M. Zielinski

Published by
WALLACE-HOMESTEAD BOOK CO.
P. O. Box BI
Des Moines, Iowa 50304

Printed in U.S.A.

Table of Contents

From "Portrait of Iowa"

Introduction

The Amish stand as a link with America's past. Charles Krault in excerpts from his *On the Road* television series commented, "There are always a saving few who make the connection between the way we are and the way we used to be." Like the Pilgrims and the Puritans, the Amish came to America in search of religious freedom and a new land in which to grow. Unlike the others, the Amish are still very much with us and so are their barn raisings, winter ice cuttings, sewing bees and many other parts of the past. Today they go on living their pioneer lives in defiance of modern man and machines and, in so doing, prosper.

To many, the Amish seem a dour, introverted people living an impossibly harsh life without electricity, tractors, insurance, government subsidies and many other "necessities" of life. This impression is one generally formed second-hand or by observing the Amish from a distance. Any visitor to one of the Amish areas will find the Amish full of curiosity about other ways of life, friendly and not without humour. And, they are happy to talk about themselves. I have seen many a modern farmer so busy in his field that he barely had time to wave. But, every Amish farmer working his land with his team of horses always had time to stop by the fence for a chat.

The clock of Amish life simply ticks at a different rate from that of the modern world. They are living, for the most part, the lives of our great-grandfathers. I have seen a wagon in the Kalona, Iowa, area with "John Deere 1905" burned into the front of the box. Take yourself back seventy years to when that wagon came from the John Deere factory: would the Amish have seemed so strange then? Most of our great-grandfathers wore beards, all of them drove wagons or buggies unless they lived in the big cities. The farming methods of the Amish were used by many others into the thirties and forties and many farmers still depend on the kerosene lantern for light.

There is nothing in the Amish way of life to inspire grimness. They live a plain life, it is true, but within the bounds of nature they can feel secure. They work with the seasons, not by the hour. The difference between an Amish buggy and a car is not just the horse in front: it can also be seen on the dashboard. In an Amish buggy you may find a calendar; in the car, a clock with the seconds ticking away.

When people grow old in Amish society, they are never cast off. They still have an active role in the family. The Amish form of social security (the Amish have not paid social security for a number of years, granted an exemption when they consistently proved they would never collect it) is a grandpa house built onto the main house. Here the parents move when their prime is past and allow the last child remaining at home to take over the main farm. But grandpa and grandma are still very much a part of the family with their house often connected by a breezeway to the main one. They help with the growing young family, which often has as many as twelve or thirteen children, and do whatever other chores they can: tending the vegetable garden, canning, quilting and a thousand other little things that always need doing.

In Amish society, everyone has his place, everyone his duties, but there is also time for fun: for singings, taffy pulls, quilting bees, summer picnics, winter ice cutting. Working together as one group much as did the early pioneers they find work and life not half so hard a chore as do some of us with all our machines, particularly with the recent gas shortages and rising food costs. More than one of us are taking a second and third look at the Amish way of life.

Because for many years the Amish in Europe were persecuted and discriminated against, they developed a life of self-sufficiency. Nearly total. It is said that an Amishman in the 1930's was asked how he felt about the Great Depression and replied, "what depression?"

In addition to growing their cash crops and raising hogs, cattle, chickens, the Amish also have sizeable vegetable gardens and much of the summer's harvest is canned or stored (like potatoes, cabbages and turnips) in root cellars. Orchards are common and if an Amish family does not have fruit trees, they will help a neighbor gather his crop and often take payment only in fruit. The Amish have learned, as did our pioneer ancestors, to live within nature. Winter brings cold, but it also brings ice and the Iowa Amish have maintained ice cutting on farm ponds to stock ice houses through the long, hot Iowa summers.

Fuel is no problem in winter for many of the Amish. They load a sled with timber from nearby woodlands and have wood enough in two or three loads for a good part of the winter. They still use sleighs so even the worst snowfall is not enough to prevent their going to church or visiting. The Old Order Amish still hold church services at different homes (on a rotating basis), a custom that evolved from the years of persecution in the early days. The lack of an established church building made it difficult to locate the Amish service and harder for the persecutors to find them. A bench wagon, looking much like an old horse-drawn hearse, carries folded benches to be set up at the individual homes for the services that, in warm weather, are held in the barns. The services themselves demand a kind of pioneer fortitude. They are often three hours long and everyone must sit on the backless benches with women separate from the men. Services are in High German, although the regular language of the Amish is a kind of German dialect liberally mixed with many English words.

The pleasures of the Amish are simple. A picnic at an Amish farm often brings out most of the Amish in an area. Threshing time when all work together can be both "business" and pleasure, for there always is time to "visit." An auction is a chance for a get-together and also an opportunity for some good bargains such as much needed farm equipment or another buggy for a young son coming of age. Ironically, in recent years the Amish often have to outbid the antique dealers for the equipment and tools the Amish still use daily. Between the bidding, there are many comments exchanged and at one auction I attended, one old Amishman nudged another who was admiring a handmade cradle, saying, "Planning something, Emery?" The Amish always have had many children and have a saying, "a new baby every spring."

The Amish way of life is not so much a strict one as a simple one. The main tenet of Amish belief is that all things must be utilitarian: clothing for covering, not adornment; shades or simple window coverings not curtains. Amish women, despite the restrictions, have found ways around this by collecting all manner of calendars (with pictures on them), having picture plates and sewing intricate designs and decorations into quilts, coverlets and pillowcases. The Amish farmyard is often filled with beautiful flowers and more share the vegetable garden's border. The Amish man can find beauty in a fine and well-cared for horse and farm land that blooms to his touch.

A friend brought me word from Minnesota of the first harvest from Amish settlers in southeastern Minnesota. One hundred bushels of oats per acre was their first yield. A farmer with modern machinery says he considers 60 bushels good. In the face of sophisticated modern farm machinery the Amish have continued to depend for the most part on the horse and horse drawn equipment. "A horse reproduces itself, a tractor produces nothing but debts," say the Amish.

My interest in the Amish dates back a dozen years when I came to the University of Iowa after four years in the Air Force, the last of which was spent in Spain and was followed by a second year of living as a Spaniard in Madrid. The result was seeing my own country with "new eyes" when I returned. America has always been called the great melting pot, but if you look closely you'll find many radically different life styles and languages existing everywhere in the United States. I started looking for places to explore on weekends and found the Amish only eighteen miles away from Iowa City. For the next few years, I stuck out my thumb whenever I got the chance and hitchiked down to the little town of Kalona. I still remember that first ride. As we topped the hill, there was an Amishman plowing with a five-horse hitch.

It is impossible to photograph a people on any continuing basis without developing a deeper interest in their way of life than you originally had. I have come to respect the Amish as a people who just about totally practice what they preach. And, today, that is a remarkable quality.

This is the country near Erlenbach, birthplace of Jacob Ammann, in the canton of Bern, Switzerland. Photo by Jan Gleysteen.

The Beginning

The Amish were born from the religious turmoil of the Anabaptist movement in 16th Century Switzerland; although, it was nearly 170 years before Jacob Ammann, a Mennonite minister and elder, disagreed with the general church rules and led his splinter group away in 1693. The church had started in 1525 when a group of men defied the established state church and published their own beliefs which included separation of church and state and adult baptism. They felt that many who were baptized as a child knew little of true faith and merely gave lip service to their religion.

The state church wasted no time in banning the new faith. From that point began a long and bloody battle of repression and extermination. The new religion was branded Ana-Baptist, a word that in the Christian world of the time suggested heathens or devil worshippers. The people called themselves the Brethren and came to be known as the Swiss Brethren and finally, Mennonites, after Menno

Above: Jacob Ammann's signature on the 1693 Document that set the Amish apart. Below: A view of the Document. Photos by Jan Gleysteen.

Simons, one of the early leaders. Felix Manz, one of the early founders, was drowned by state authorities on January 5, 1527. He was followed to his death by many simple people who embraced the faith: the farmer, the cobbler, the butcher, the carpenter, the housewife and mother. They faced the bonfire, garrotting or beheading—at the worst. At the best, tortures that left them maimed for life if they did not recant their faith.

The new faith forbade them to swear an oath of alliegiance to the government, for they believed man owed allegiance only to God. They did not believe in war or any other violent act and, for this, they were subjected to the extreme violence of death. In one town there were so many "heretics" caught that a huge bonfire was built in the town square to accommodate all the "offenders." To make things easy, they were tied to long ladders and dropped one by one into the flames. At first, executions were public, but the authorities soon discovered such an event only served to increase the numbers of converts. Instead, they began executing "heretics" quietly; drowning by being held face down in a barrel was a favorite method for it also left no marks on the body. Nearly a thousand died for their faith before the death penalty for this "offense" was abolished in 1571.

The Martry's Mirror, a collection of accounts of martyrs starting with the early Christians to the 1500's, was published in 1660. Today, the *Bible*, the *Martyr's Mirror* and the *Ausbund*, one of the oldest of Protestant hymnals, are the three most important books of the Amish.

Thun Castle in canton Bern where the Amish were imprisoned in 1711 prior to being deported to Holland. Photo by Jan Gleysteen.

From the *Martyrs Mirror;* Torture of Geleyn the Shoemaker.

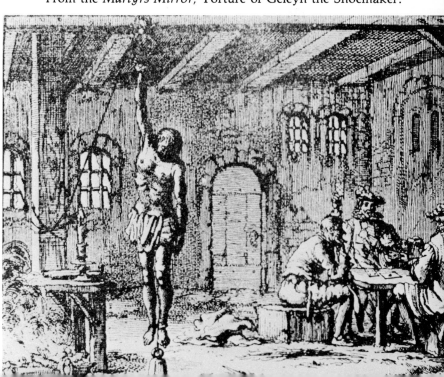

From the *Martyrs Mirror:* Jan Woutress and Adriaenken Jans burned.

From the *Martyrs Mirror:* Martyrdom of Anneken Heyndricks.

From the *Martyrs Mirror:* Mattheus Mair's steadfastness.

The writings in the *Martyr's Mirror* consist mainly of letters and accounts written by the condemned themselves and the following is quite representative:

> "O my dearest love on earth, kiss all my children once for me, and tell my Susan that it is her father's wish that she be obedient to her mother in the fear of God."

The Swiss Brethren continued to grow stronger and although they were no longer put to death, they were still tortured and banished. If the banished member returned and was again captured, he might be sold as a galley slave in Italy. Soon, even these punishments were halted, but even when the ashes of the last martyrs had long blown away, the Brethren still were not allowed to live as they chose. They could not own land, were forbidden to live in cities and could not be apprenticed to learn a trade. Their young people found it difficult to obtain permission to marry. Into this world Jacob Ammann was born February 12, 1644 in Erlenbach, canton of Bern, Switzerland. His influence as a religious leader has spanned over three hundred years. It is because of his teachings that the Amish still speak German, hold services in High German, dress in the simplest manner and live a plain life. As you can see by the drawing included in this section, the Amish of the earlier period were not as simply dressed as today.

By 1711 the Swiss government had run out of patience with the Ana-Baptists. Many Amish and Mennonites were imprisoned. When it became too expensive to feed them, they were loaded on ships and sent to Holland (which, then, was a liberal country regarding religion). They had to forfeit all their possessions and start anew. By 1750, the Amish, who originated in the canton of Bern, Switzerland in 1693, were gone. They scattered through central Europe to Germany, France, Holland and into Russia, but it was only in America (where they began migrating after 1700) that they were to grow and prosper. Jacob Ammann was never to find peace in his lifetime. He had moved his flock to Alsace, an independent state which later became part of France, but in 1712 he and his followers were expelled. Such was the fate of the Amish in Europe, to be consistently shuttled from one country to another, to be taxed and forbidden to own land, to be harassed in one way or another until they disappeared from Europe entirely. At first, they feared migrating to America: the long ocean voyage was dangerous and they had heard about the "wild Indians" who lived there. But a few did move. The journey to America was to be the Amish's survival.

THE JOURNEY

Although three hundred Amish made the journey to America before the Revolutionary War, it was only after the American Constitution was ratified that they came in large numbers. For generations, the Amish tried to find a permanent home in Europe, but each new country proved only a temporary haven. The American Constitution guaranteed freedom of religion to all, not just Catholics, Lutherans, but to all. And the second great attraction was land: plentiful and cheap. They had always been renters in Europe. In America, they could own the land.

Jacob Hochstetler is one of the earliest Amish settlers for whom there is a ship's record. He arrived in Philadelphia Sept. 1, 1736 on the ship *Harle* from Rotterdam. It is likely that there were other Amish here as early as 1713. But the fate of the Jacob Hochstetler family may have been one of the reasons early migration was delayed, for the story did reach the Amish in Europe. Hochstetler had come with his wife and young son and, perhaps, one more child. The French and Indian War broke out in 1754 and on September 19, 1757 the Hochstetler farm was attacked. The son, Jacob, and a daughter were tomahawked and scalped, the mother stabbed to death and Jacob and his sons, Christian and Joseph taken captive. Jacob eventually escaped and, many years later, the sons were returned. Unfortunately, this was a familiar story along the frontier.

It was not until after 1800 that the Amish began coming in earnest. From the family record of Abraham C. Nisly comes the story of his voyage to America. He went aboard ship on June 6, 1804 although the voyage did not get underway until the ship had a full passenger load on July 2. It did not reach the open sea until July 17 and then was captured by a British Man O' War. The seizure was partly due, undoubtedly, to the impressment of seamen into the British Navy, a practice that climaxed with the War of 1812. As a result, the ship did not arrive in Philadelphia until October 12, 1804. Nisly was a redempter and redempters could not leave ship until someone came to pay for the passage. A notice from a Lancaster, Pa. newspaper for September 10, 1801, affords the best explanation of the practice:

> "A number still on board the ship *Anna* from Hamburg, Germany, lying abreast of Vine Street wharf (Philadelphia) consisting of mechanics of every description, farmers and others. Their time will be disposed of at the low rate of $80 for their passage."

They were servants, not slaves. The adults generally worked for four or five years to repay their "benefactor." Children usually until they were 21 years old. Christian, as he came to be commonly called, appears to have been one of these servants. Later, he married and settled in Holmes County, Ohio and became the father of fourteen children.

The dress of the couple on the left is typical of the Alsatian Amish around 1815. You will notice that their dress is somewhat more ornate than Amish dress of today although it strongly resembles that of the Mifflin Co. Amish to be seen in the next section.

A more detailed account of the voyage across the Atlantic is found in a diary kept by Daniel Guengerich who left Germany with his mother, step-father, brother and half-brothers and sisters in 1833:

"On the 9th of May, 1833, we started on the great journey. (They traveled by boat down the river Weser to Bremen). Since we had so early sent our earnest-money there we believed confidently that we could go aboard ship immediately. But it was no different here than at Muenden. The larger the company of emigrants and the more frequently they arrive here, likewise the longer seamen can detain them here . . . the better it suits the innkeepers and merchants of Bremen.

". . . Late in the evening of the 29th we went aboard and also sailed off, but on account of stormy weather and antagonistic winds we could not even reach the end of the city . . .

"On the morning of the 31st before daybreak . . . another boat had torn loose and came so close to ours that the sailors could not entirely prevent a mighty collision . . . we received such a strong jar that the anchor chain broke and now both ships were committed to the force of the stream whereupon the skipper of the other boat started a great lamentation in which he pulled out his hair . . ."

Apparently, things were righted for by June 5th, the ship was underway, more or less:

"On June 5th toward noon we had a strong west wind right against us causing the ship to lie sometimes on its right side and then its left . . .

"On the 6th . . . at evening we saw France on the left side and England on the right . . .

"If we had good winds, we could have made this 18-day trip to the Atlantic Ocean, where we are now, in four days . . .

"On Sunday, the 28th (July), we had west wind and in the morning, rain . . . in the evening we got a thunder storm with strong tempest and thunder and lightning such as we seldom have on land, also heavy showers so that we collected several barrels of water for we had a water shortage . . ."

On August 12, they made port in Baltimore, 72 days after coming aboard ship and 94 days after they had left their home.

Many of those who managed to pay for their passage had little or no money when they landed. When 17-year-old Jacob Gingerich arrived in Baltimore he had only 25 cents in his pocket. The Daniel Benders arrived penniless and began a 27 mile walk to their son's home. They were helped along by a kindly farmer. The important thing was that they had arrived in a new land of promise where their beliefs would not get them thrown in prison or taxed beyond all means to pay.

And so the Amish began to grow and spread across the Americas.

ONE MAN'S JOURNEY
by Jan Gleysteen

In the early 1880's, life was pretty difficult for the Mennonites and Amish of Central Europe. Although they were no longer being killed for their faith, other forms of persecution continued. They were not allowed to own land, they faced harassment from the state church officials, and often had to pay double taxes for the "privilege" of being different. In addition there were wars which caused the loss of life and destruction of property.

In 1821, Christian Nafziger, a 45-year-old Amishman, who lived not far from Munich in Bavaria, Germany, had his rent increased to the point where he could no longer provide for his family. That same summer he decided to go and see whether somewhere in this world there would be a better place for him, his family and the other Amish of Bavaria and the Alsace. So he said good-bye to his dear family, picked up his cane and wandered off into the unknown.

After many long days of walking, Chris came to Amsterdam, Holland, a distance of 570 miles from home, where he was kindly received by the Dutch Mennonites. Upon hearing Christian's story, one Mennonite merchant, Brother van Eeghen, wrote a check for fifty dollars to the order of the Vincent Holte Shipping Co. for Christian's passage on a sailing vessel to North America.

The ship docked in New Orleans in January 1822. After figuring that the fare amounted to $40 (based on food and supplies actually used) he received $10 back plus a gift of $10 from Mr. Nolte, the ship's owner, who had become sympathetic to the needs of Nafziger and the Amish. With these twenty dollars, Christian Nafziger took his cane and headed north. He walked more than a thousand miles to Philadelphia and from there on west to Lancaster. The Lancaster Mennonite settlers shared their homes with him and upon his departure gave him an old horse on which to continue his journey. Christian Nafziger arrived in Upper Canada (now Ontario) in August, 1822. In Upper Canada Christian visited Governor Maitland to find out whether the governor would be willing to sell some of the newly opened lands to his people. He found out that the governor was indeed very much interested in having them come to Canada. He promised to reserve for the Amish some virgin forests of pine, oak and maple from the Crown Reserves west of Waterloo, laid out in 200-acre lots. (Today this area is called Wilmot).

Naturally Christian was very excited about the possibility of Amish owning land of their own. His only concern was where to get the money to bring his people across the ocean. But he also knew that the Lord would show them a way. And already the Waterloo County Mennonites were collecting money for his own voyage home. Thankful for this, and anxious to share the good news at home, he marched off toward New York City at once.

From New York he sailed to London. Here he stopped to see King George IV of England to discuss his agreement with Governor Maitland. In simple words, Brother Nafziger told him of the plight of the Amish in Bavaria and of their desire for a home of their own in a land of freedom. His Majesty was touched by this story and promised Christian and his family, and all who would follow him to Canada, fifty acres of land free per family out of the lots they would buy. The king then pressed several pieces of gold in his hand and wished him a safe journey home. After sailing across the North Sea Christian Nafziger walked along the Rhine River and from there on east into Bavaria where he found his family just as poor but in good health in January, 1823.

Once home, Christian wrote a letter to the brothers and sisters in Upper Canada in which he described their continuing hardships in Bavaria, and expressed that their only way out was to trust in the Lord, who'd show all of them the way to Canada as lovingly and as certainly as he had already personally experienced his own long voyage.

When this letter arrived the Ebytown Mennonites organized to collect funds which they forwarded to Philadelphia in payment for the passage of the Amish. When this good news reached Nafziger he immediately shared it with the brotherhood. In the spring of 1823 the first wagons began rolling toward Rotterdam and Le Havre. The Dutch Mennonites opened their homes to the travelers and generously contributed toward the migration expenses. And across the ocean these pioneers found the Canadian money waiting for them. The Amish saw this as an answer to their prayers. During the next several years more Amish continued to sail from Europe.

Christian Nafziger himself, his wife, three sons and two daughters followed in the spring of 1826. Christian experienced another example of God's leading in their migration. While in Philadelphia they became acquainted with a Mennonite family from Bucks County, Pa., who invited them to their home to rest up from the ocean voyage. Those friendly Mennonites sent them off to Canada with fresh supplies and a new wagon on which they reached Upper Canada in October 1826.

After spending the winter with the Mennonite settlers at Ebytown the Nafzigers took possession of their chosen lot in Wilmot. After clearing the land and building their required section of highway they built a house. Unfortunately Christian's wife passed away before the house was finished. Christian himself died ten years later.

Across the Americas

A question often asked about the Amish is: Can their way of life survive? After having visited many of the Amish settlements across this country I believe that they can and will survive—not entirely without change—already in many states the tractor is being used side by side with the horse. But since the first Amish came to America over 250 years ago they have changed little in their beliefs and their general life style.

Today there are 112 Amish settlements. The southernmost is Asuncion, Paraguay as the Amish continue their pioneering ways in the search for more good farmland for their sons. The most western settlement is Hutchinson, Kansas although there had been settlements in Oregon and New Mexico. The northernmost settlement is Wadena, Minnesota. In North America the easternmost settlement is Norfolk, New York. Of the present settlements 73 per cent were established after 1940. Only 17 per cent of the settlements were established before 1900.

The Amish came to this country in great number after 1800 during the Napoleonic Wars and marched steadily westward into Ohio, Indiana, Illinois, Iowa and Nebraska. Today they can be found in Delaware, Florida, Illinois, Indiana, Iowa, Kansas, Kentucky, Maryland, Michigan, Minnesota, Missouri, New York, Ohio, Oklahoma, Pennslyvania, Tennessee, Virginia, Wisconsin, Honduras Paraquay and Canada.

LANCASTER, PENN. It was in Berks and Lancaster that the Amish first came in the early 1700's. Today despite tourist buses on all sides they continue with their normal activity. The shots above and to the left were taken on the main Highway into Intercouse. Tourists seemed to pay them little heed as they headed for the tourist attraction ahead and the Amish tours.

30

THE BUDGET

LANCASTER, PA.

July 10—Church services in Smoketown district on Sun. were held at Enos Fisher's instead of David Beiler's, as Lizzie was in the hospital a week. She had walking pneumonia; came home the beginning of this week. Then early this morning she wanted to start fire to heat water for the washing, and after putting kerosene on, it burned too much and set fire to the wash-house. The interior of the wash house was burned a good bit, and the sink and cabinet area just inside the kitchen door was badly charred, but the rest of the house had mostly just smoke damage.

Above: Here a water wheel at Lancaster provides power for pumping water and other chores. The Amish have long been able to make use of the natural resources provided by God rather than to depend on the power sources of man.

Below: Not all the Amish got the best land in Pennslyvania. These boys are picking up rocks from a newly plowed field near Springs in Somerset Co. The first Amish church group was formed there in 1772.

THE BUDGET

SILVER SPRING, PA.
O.O.R.B.

Aug. 27—Greetings! This past week has been another fun week and we are grateful for the blessings of friends and fruits of the earth. We ladies have been canning and freezing foods from the garden. We have had some extremely hot days and then cooler days with showers of rain, which refreshed everything.

SPRINGS, PENN. Almost never will you see buggy or wagon on the road without children along. Below: A little Amish boy wears his dress until he is out of the diaper stage as did all children of the turn of the century and before.

DOVER, DELAWARE. Above: The Amishman who owns the buggy to the left of the children obviously has a sense of humour, as he has fastened the lettering from a Ford Fairlane to the back of his buggy. Below: You will notice that the Amish buggies are not all alike, neither are the customs of various Amish communities. You will find buggies with different configurations, bonnets of different styles and even suspenders that are different.

Preceding Page: Outside Strasburg in Lancaster these Amish load bundles of oats in preparation for threshing.

BELLEVILLE, MIFFLIN CO., PENN. Home of two Amish splinter groups, the white buggy and yellow buggy groups. Below: Notice that the dress is quite different from that of the average Amish women.

MIFFLIN CO., PENN. By the 1790's the Amish were settling in the Kishacoquillas Valley. Here two splinter groups formed which were much more strict in their interpretations of Jacob Ammann's rules. Ammann believed in nonconformity to social customs and stressed the importance of untrimmed beards and the plainest possible clothes and headgear. In all the other Amish areas I have visited I was able to talk with the Amish and compare them and their customs with others I had talked with, but this Amish group would not talk. I was lucky to have a man whose mother came from that particular group stop in to talk with me when I returned home.

Lewis Miller who is a 90-year-old Mennonite minister had returned to his mother's people a number of times over the years in order to prepare a book on

this group. This group froze its dress and its church customs at the time of the Revolutionary War. The church service resembles the Quakers more than other Amish groups as the men sit in church with their hats on through most of the service. The noon meal which they eat together after church is dill pickles, a large slice of dark bread and a large mug of coffee and nothing more. The women never adopted the bonnets that stand today as the symbol of Amish women. The windmill, symbol of most Amish farms, is also absent from their farms. "God provides us with the water; we shouldn't ask him to pump it too," one of this group said. The women's dress are all ankle-length and the prayer caps they wear remind me of the kind of clothes that were worn in the 18th century.

MIFFLIN Co., Penn. Above: Farm without windmill. Below: Dress of this branch of Amish is quite different from the ordinary.

THE BUDGET

KALONA, IOWA

August 20—The rains have now come. We had nearly three inches of rain, already this week. The lawns are getting green again.

Jars, jars, jars. That is what we have setting in the wash house since this evening. One of our egg customers had asked if I could use some fruit jars. She knew of a place where they had some old canned things and they had intended to haul it all to the dump, but she told them that jars are too valuable to throw away. My jars were getting pretty well all filled so I said I could use some. She came with box after box after box of them. So now I'll have dumping and cleaning and sterilizing to do and if I can find lids I'll have plenty of jars to can the rest of our fruit, with also some jars to spare.

OELWEIN, IOWA. Above: A young Amish mother in Iowa with typical Amish dress. Below: Hitchrail in Kalona, Iowa.

NEW WILMINGTON, PENN. This group was an offshoot of the Amish from Mifflin Co. and their buggies were all burnt orange in color. Although the dress of the women is more typical of the other Amish people, it is dark brown instead of the traditional black.

Preceding Pages: Here a typical Iowa Amish girl (From "Portrait of Iowa") in contrast to one from Mifflin Co.

CONEWANGO VALLEY, NEW YORK. Above: A buggy winds its way along the back country road that leads to the Amish area. This area was settled in 1949 and only in 1974 two new settlements started in the northeastern part of the state.

Below: A typical Amish farm house from the New York area. Notice the benches piled on the front porch. Amish "church" was held there the past Sunday and they are stacked ready to be taken to the next Amish home for church.

Corn planting in the Conewango Valley.

THE BUDGET

CONEWANGO VALLEY, N.Y.

June 7—Jacob J. Wengerd's had several frolics last week to build a new shop and put roofing on their house.

Dan Raber will soon be having his barn raising.

Joe E. Millers and Joe E. Swartzentrubers both have frolics planned for next week to put other roofs on their houses

Above: Corn being cultivated near Kalona, Iowa. A son works with his father to learn farming.

WAYNE-HOLMES COUNTIES, OHIO. Above and below: This Amish boy dresses in a style more typical of the cowboy with tight jeans and a cowboy hat.

Above: Maysville, Ohio. Amishmen bring in a wagon load of corn.

Below: Just outside Fredericksburg, Ohio.

THE BUDGET

FAIRBANK, IOWA
[Buchanan County]

June 12—Had some rain yesterday. Had been cool for the last week. Hay is ready to cut, looks like a heavy crop. Some corn is about knee high already and fields seem to be clean this year.

Next page: Spring plowing near Kalona, Iowa.

INDIANA. Above: A young father shows his son how to drive.

Below: One of the many buggy shops that can be found around the Amish areas.

Preceding Page: This Amishman is sowing oats near Kitchner-Waterloo in Ontario, Canada. His family was one of the early settlers who came to Canada in the 1820's.

THE BUDGET

NAPPANEE, IND.

July 16—Mrs. Edward Chupp broke her collarbone and had to have stitches to close a cut on her head when she had an accident this week one evening. She was riding on a bike and leading a horse, when the horse got scared of a combine in the field and made a jerk and threw her on the hardtop road.

Above: A scene typical of many of the small towns in the northeastern part of Indiana and southern part of Michigan.

Below: Indiana is also the only state to require buggy licenses. Each buggy must have a license plate. They are designated non-motor vehicles.

Next page: Young Amish boy discing near Alymer, Ontario, Canada. Most of the Amish in this group came to Canada in recent years from the United States.

THE BUDGET

WROXETER, ONT., CAN.
(Gorrie District)

Aug. 25—Rain, rain, rain. We got over 5 inches of it Saturday night. Sunday it rained again and now today we had a shower, too. Not very good second crop hayin' weather.

Thrashing is in full swing.

Wonder if Orva Hochstetler will get his wife a coon hound now, since his encounter with one last week one night. He had gotten up during the night and heard something in the kitchen, then heard a lamp chimney fall and break in the stainless steel sink. He yelled at his wife to bring a flashlight or something and about that time something furry brushed against his leg & went out the doorway.

They only have a blanket over the doorway yet on their new addition of the house. They figure it was a coon or maybe a stray cat, but Orva thinks more likely a coon as the fur he felt, felt more stiff like a coon's rather than a cat. He said it sure makes one's hair stand on end anyway.

51

THE BUDGET

MEYERSDALE, PA.

Greetings. Health seems on the mend again. Hay season is here with some starting, others putting in grass for silage, a bumper crop.

People are now looking forward to cherry day. There is an orchard near Somerset with 32 different kinds of apples, many of the old timers.

When I worked at Hans Yoders we picked apples all fall. He had 3 farms and 4 good orchards.

In the winter we started apples and peddled them in the mining towns, ready sale $1.00 bu., at that time, the mines were working full time, and we nearly always had good coal.

I wonder if any one, has good clover honey, for sale? Or other clear, orange blossom is good, but too far away.

THE BUDGET

CASHTON, WISC.
Monroe & Vernon Counties

June 1—Lots of corn went in the ground the last week. Oats and hay and wheat are growing nicely. Some corn is big enough to cultivate.

South church was at Wm. Kempfs today. Young folks singing is to be there this eve.

Wm. Schmuckers had a frolic Friday to add to their barn for horse stables. They must have had a good turn out as they got the roof on the first day. Levi W. Millers want to have frolics this week to take the roof off of their house and build an up-stairs on, as it is just a one-story house.

JAMESPORT, MISSOURI. In the last few years Missouri has added a number of new Amish settlements. They began settling in Jamesport in 1953.

Above: Amish boys on way to help their father with haying.

Below: Amish buggy with mud flap added for muddy Missouri roads.

Preceding page: This Amish man was cutting oats. Talking with him, I found that he had recently moved to Jamesport from near Hutchison, Kansas where he had grown up using tractors and combines. He moved to Missouri because he wanted to get back to old fashioned horse farming.

THE BUDGET

BOWLING GREEN, MO.

July 31—Weather is still warm and dry. Born to Willard S. and Katie W. (Eicher) Bontrager a son named Jacob, on July 26, greeted by 6 sisters and 4 brothers.

Rudy, age 5, son of Willard S. Bontragers fell from a teeter totter while playing with his neighbor boys and broke his arm. He was given attention in the Dr's. office and returned home the same evening.

HUTCHINSON, KANSAS. These pictures were taken around the small town of Yoder just outside Hutchinson. Here the old order Amish began using tractors in 1937 because their wheat farms had to be much larger than the typical Amish farm of 80 to 100 acres. Also the wheat had to be harvested in the hottest Kansas weather when temperatures were around 100 and horses died from heat exhaustion. The Amish adapted to the situation.

KALONA, IOWA. The scenes on these two pages are typical of many of the smaller towns across the United States with Amish surrounding them.

ARTHUR, ILLINOIS. Arthur, Illinois is one of the most typical Amish towns. Every Friday they have a farmers market where they sell home-canned goods, fresh fruits and vegetables and bakery goods. I talked to an Amish farmer from this area and found that the Amish were buying out other farmers as they retire so as the years go by it will become even more Amish.

THE BUDGET

BIRD-IN-HAND, PA.

Sept. 5—We have nice growing weather and farmers are cutting tobacco but some of it is rusty. Peaches are also plentiful, also lima beans.

These Amish boys take it easy after Sunday church services. After over three hours on hard benches they need to relax a little.

THE BUDGET

MIDDLEFIELD, OHIO
Newcomb Road Area

Sept. 19—Still very wet. Menfolks are plowing ground for fall planting, and filling silos whenever they can get in the corn fields. Yesterday we had an all day rain which was probably rather unpleasant for the wedding goings-on at Albert M. Troyers, for their daughter, Becky, to John (Dan J.) Troyer.

Still sore throats, colds and earaches among the children, and also an ornery stomach upset lasting about 24 hours, affecting any age, even me.

Mahlon Yoder baptismal services were very well attended. I think most of John J. Miller's northeast Troy church were present, as two of their young folds were also baptised there. Crist R. Hershberger had the anfang, John J. Miller the main part of preaching, and Mahlon (Bish.) Yoder did the baptizing part. That church is to be at Dan O. Millers on Shedd Rd. next time, council meeting, Sept. 28th.

The Oil drillers have come and gone from across the road. It took just a little over a week to go down about 4500 feet. This rig moved to Dan C. (Betsy) Bylers, down the road from us. In the meantime, 2 more rigs moved to Noah Masts and Crist E. Millers, not far apart. So there is quite a humming and lots of traffic in this neighborhood right now, and the three towers lit up, look almost like big Christmas trees to the children, who are very excited about the whole business.

Levi S. Yoders, Noah D. Millers, Lester E. Mullets, and probably others are planning to go to Stark Co. tomorrow, to an auction sale at Levi's daughter Gertie, the Levi A. Millers.

Roman J. Schmuckers also intend to have a small sale tomorrow p.m. to sell some surplus household goods, that they don't have any room for, in their smaller house.

We hear that there are about a dozen families planning to move to Clymer, New York, just beyond the Pa. line, and start a new settlement there. Guess I'd better not try and name them yet, as I may have been misinformed.

This is an Amish school west of Kitchener-Waterloo, Ontario, Canada, in the area settled by the Amish in the 1820's. Their dress is quite atypical of the majority of the Amish which allows colors but usually only in subdued pastels. These Amish children were wearing the brightest reds, greens, yellows and oranges that I have ever seen.

THE BUDGET

PARIS, TENNESSEE

March 27—Isn't spring a wonderful time of the year? How can anyone say there is no God after witnessing the rebirth of the many flowers and trees.

March has surely been wet and cool. Upon checking our potatoes that we'd planted, we discovered the majority were rotten. So it doesn't always pay to plant real early. Peas and other early seed are peeking through.

Sunday we had council meetings and we'll have communion on Easter Sunday. Good Friday will be a day of prayer and meditation. We hope all may receive a special blessing this Easter Season. How foolish t'would be to celebrate with egg hunts, bunnys, baby chicks, etc. Where did such paganism begin?

These children from Aylmer, Ontario are much more typical of Amish school children. Their color scheme was very conservative. Since the Supreme Court ruled in favor of Amish parochial schools a great many new ones have been built across the United States.

THE BUDGET

KALONA, IOWA

November 1—We had nearly 2 inches of rain this week and mild weather.

Churches on the 10th are to be at Lester B. Millers, Wallace Bontragers and Henry H. Yoders.

On Wednesday evening, Elmer C. Millers, Joe F. Millers and Wilbur Ropps were here to help snitz apples. The next day I made 6 gallon apple butter. The egg customers also readily buy homemade apple butter, even tho the sugar is over 40 cents a pound.

On Tuesday, Mrs. Eli A. Swartzendruber had an all day quilting, with a pot luck dinner at noon. Her quilters were all that were born in the same year, with 17 being present.

Dea. Jonas Masts and daughter, Lewis Kauffmans and Menno Yoders of Jamesport, Mo. and Menno Hochstetlers of Milton spent a night in this community, last week, on their way home from Cashton, Wis. where they had attended a 1-W meeting.

The market place in Alymer, Ontario, Canada.

THE BUDGET

AYLMER, ONT., CAN.

June 13—The young folks had a gathering on Tuesday evening to clean and sand the church benches. It's surprising how much wear and usage they get in a few years time. The next day the women varnished them.

A Pioneer Heritage

The Amish learned well the need for self-reliance. Over the years they found themselves on the frontiers of this developing nation and in the remotest areas to be found in most states. They like their lives of isolation—far away from the devil of big city influences.

While the rest of America has pursued the great American Dream of More—filling brand new homes with brand new appliances of every size and description, the Amish continued to buy what they needed, the necessities rather than the luxuries. Today while the garbage piles high in the streets of larger cities, that have become telephone pole jungles unsafe to live in—the Amish continue working in mutual pioneer co-operation. If a newly married couple needs a house, they all get together to help him build it. If a neighbor is sick and can't do his farm chores, the neighbors come over and help out until he is well. In this way there are no great strains on the Amish budget, even though the actual cash earned in a given year might be small in our terms. We civilized people often find ourselves working more hours to pay for the conveniences which the Amish do without.

The Amish world is made refreshing by its lack of complexity, confusion and haste. A young child quickly learns what is expected of him or her. The child quickly becomes a working member of the team

THE BUDGET

Monday afternoon the girls were rolling logs onto the skids at the mill. Somehow 2 logs rolled together, causing Carolyn's kaut hook handle to fly back on her head in front of the ear, causing a concussion.

Thursday the menfolks got together and put up the walls, Celotex and some of the rafters on Rudy Wickey's new house. Yesterday the rafters were finished and about half the roof put on.

THE BUDGET
SALEM, IND.

Jan. 18—The young folks got to skate a few days this week, but after the rain last night, there is water on the pond this morning.

Nicholas Stoltzfuses had the young folks for supper and singing Sunday evening. Quite a few children were sick with flu and missing from school this week.

Getting ready to go home from school, teacher Christian Wanner tied his horse to an old desk outside the schoolhouse and went in to get the saddle. The desk moved, disturbing the horse more and they both went flying thru the pasture, bits of desk flying off till little was left when Leo caught him close to the mill yard.

and from the time he begins to understand is given little tasks to do. I have yet to meet an Amishman who couldn't spare time out from plowing or other farm chores to chat a half hour or so with a passerby. The strength of their life has been proven by their prosperity. They teach that work itself is good and can be quite enjoyable. Despite the fact that they work with their hands and with *real* horsepower, their farms continue to be successful.

I talked with an Amishman in Jamesport, Missouri who gave me his interpretation of the difference between the Amish and the rest of us. "You are materialists. You want what you want because you want it. We are utilitarians. If we need something new it is adopted into our ways." He cited as an example his own upbringing near Hutchison, Kansas. The Amish farmers there had to adopt the use of tractors and combines as far back as 1937. Kansas is a wheat state and wheat must be harvested at the hottest time of the year. The horses were dying from exhaustion, so the tractor and combines came into use, yet the horse is still very much a part of their life. The wheat once harvested is carried to the grain elevators in horse drawn wagons, the horse and buggy is still their main means of transportation. They adopted only as much mechanization as necessary to survive in that location.

The secret of Amish life, if it can be called a secret, is that as much as possible they live completely in tune with nature and their environment. Those early years of persecution—backed up by constant readings from the Martyr's Mirror—keep constantly before them the idea that the fittest must survive. So the Amish are not without change. Each little Amish area has its own set of changes that may make it different from the next area. The differences can be small ones—the wearing of one style prayer cap or wearing suspenders with just one strap or two or a more basic one such as an interpretation of scripture. "Be not conformed to this world" Romans 12:2, one of Jacob Amman's basic tenets has probably caused more dissent than any other. It leaves room for a wide interpretation and this is exactly what has happened. In some Amish areas the houses remain unpainted, in others nicely painted—in other areas such as Mifflin Co., Penn., even the windmill was considered "too worldly" a device to be used, but to "outsiders" the windmill stands as the very symbol of most Amish farms.

We have already seen what rising electrical prices and shortages of gasoline can do to the American people—to most of us that is. Although the Amish have begun to use gas operated freezers and refrigerators, they have still not forgotten how to use nature's refrigeration.

On these pages are the Amish of today cutting ice in the manner our ancestors did. These large blocks of ice, some weighing almost 200 pounds will be packed in sawdust and straw and placed in ice houses. They will provide refrigeration until sometime in September or

THE BUDGET

BARNETT, MISSOURI

Feb. 13—The thermometer is hovering near the freezing point the last few days. Rain has fallen which the cool air has turned to a thin film of ice; but not enough to make driving hazardous. Some good skating was enjoyed by the young folks on the Brubaker's new pond on Sunday.

The bell on top of the school house had been frozen fast one morning when the teacher came to ring it. A few hard pulls sent forth answering peals loud enough to bring the school into session.

THE BUDGET

THOMAS, OKLA.

Jan. 17—Weatherwise we have no complaints. We got over last weekend which had pushed the mercury down to 13 above but we have had several days of 50 degree weather since then.

Farmers have been top dressing their wheat. Some cotton is to be harvested but quite a bit of it is being done this week.

October, depending on how hot the summer is. With fresh cream from the cow they have the makings of ice cream. This is but one of the many ways the Amish continue to live in a pioneer fashion.

As many as 60 Amishmen may gather in this co-operative ice cutting effort, bringing what tools they have plus horses and wagons. I counted over 20 wagons waiting to be loaded at this ice cutting and I'm sure many of them made several trips to nearby farms. The next day they would be moving to yet another farm pond to continue cutting. The one improvement they had over old time ice cutting was the addition of a gasoline powered saw mounted on a sled. They are allowed to use gasoline motors in most Amish communities, provided they do not actually drive any vehicle. Although this, too, is falling away in some Amish communities where steel-wheeled tractors are in use. In others rubber-tired tractors have been accepted. In all, the Amish have never been without change—it is only that they have carefully chosen what changes to make instead of blindly accepting all that was offered them.

The ice cutting today is more than a symbol among the Amish of their independence from the general economic system than an actual attempt to live totally in an old way. But if it were ever necessary to return to the old ways—they are the storehouse of such knowledge.

Every Amish farmer knows something of the butchering and preparing of his own meats, grinding his own grain—all things necessary to his survival without the system.

Even the heavy winter snows will not paralyze the Amish way of life as it does most of us before the complicated system of street and highway machinery goes to work. A heavy winter snow brings out the sled and the sleigh and they are off across country to visit a neighbor or attend church. The increasing price of oil, coal and other fuels does not have as much effect on the Amish, because many of them still burn wood for fuel. A sled will carry a good sized load of wood from the nearest stand of trees. The sled or a team of horses with log chains can also haul in heavy logs to be cut up for next spring's building project.

Barn Raising

One of the best examples of pioneer team work was the cabin and barn raising. To my knowledge the Amish are the only ones still to carry on this tradition. If a farmer's barn burns down his neighbors gather up what tools and lumber they have on hand and help him build it up again. This is true not only of barns, but also of houses and many other activities which require cooperation.

I have had little chance to photograph pioneer style barn raisings. In my area, as in many others, the Amish have switched to the material at hand and have been building with concrete block and metal roofs or even putting up a metal building. But in Ohio and Pennsylvania they still do it the old-fashioned way. I was lucky enough to get from Fred J. Wilson of Massilon, Ohio, permission to use his picture of an Amish barn raising and information on the event. Mr. Wilson is now preparing a book on Ohio barn raisings.

The Ohio barn raisings are truly in the pioneer style. The proper trees are selected from a stand of timber near the new barn's location. If a stream or river is nearby the Amish will actually float the logs downriver; otherwise, the logs must be hauled to the site by horsepower. A sawmill is set up and all the timber and most of the lumber is then sawed right on the spot. These barns are framed with heavy timbers and pegged and notched—that is, the main framework is put into place without the use of nails. Without the aid of cranes or power sources other than simple pullies, huge six by six timbers are hefted into places. These huge barns which can be seen across Ohio and Pennsylvania are raised in less than a day by as many as 200 men. While the men are busy on the barn the women prepare a huge noon meal. By evening the Amish will have departed for home leaving a huge barn standing where before none stood. Their pay for such a day's work is the knowledge that should they need such a barn built each man there can depend on the help of his neighbors.

The Amish are justly proud of their workmenship. They buy the best hammers and other tools designed to last a lifetime. They build their houses and barns to last for generations.

THE BUDGET

MAUGANSVILLE, MD.
Hagerstown Fellowship

August 27—We've been having some very hot weather again. The ground is getting quite dry too, although there is still moisture underneath the top soil.

Work is progressing at Abram Shanks on the new barn that is being built to replace the one that burned, having been struck by lightning. Some men escaped serious injury when some partly burned beams fell while in the cleaning up process. The pile of hay that was hauled out in the field is still smoking.

Among the plain people in the area there is quite a bit of stealing. Some have had their houses broken into, canned goods stolen and other things. Also gasoline is being taken. Wickedness seems to be abounding in many ways..

Mr. and Mrs. Merle Longberry of Townville, Pa. were vistors at Freeman Coblentzes for a few days last week. They went fishing a bit here and there. They also went to Sauble Beach one day. Freemie Jr. and family live there, as Freemie does carpentery there. While in that area, they saw a fireplace in a house, made of stone, which caught their eye, so they hunted around a bit and finally got a whole van load of stones to take home to Pa. to build a fireplace for Longberrys. Such beautiful stones I've never seen before. Some really glittered and sparkled.

THE BUDGET

MEYERSDALE, PA.

June 9—Fruit is hanging on plenty heavy, looks like it needs thinned later on unless a storm sets in. Strawberries are ripening.

I wonder how canning is to be done? With jar lids hard to get, one of our grocery store owners told me they are delivering to the south first and then up here.

Cherries should soon be ready. There were more people in the cherry orchard last year than had been for some years back.

MEYERSDALE, PA.

Aug. 20—We are having fall clouds. Our temperature dropped from 95 to 70 during the day and at night it dropped from 70 to 42 and we had a good soaking rain.

Everything is growing. Farmers are combining, threshing and making second crop hay. Hay prices at the barn average $40 to $45 per ton. Good alfalfa of course is more. Oats is a good crop. Joel Brenneman's spelty yielded 80 bu. per acre.

Visitors in Somerset Co. were Verna (Kinsinger) Miller and I believe a John Miller from Plain City, Ohio, visited her sisters, Fannie and Mary Kinsinger. We had Iowa visitors on Monday.

Meyersdale Fair is on this week with heavy traffic. Coal trucks were going at 5 this morning. Soft coal is $20 to $30 at the tipple. Some difference to what it was in 1918 and in the 20's, when it was $1.50 to $2.50 at the mines. That was deep mined coal now it is all strip mined, about 15 percent slate rock.

The grandsons are helping Amos Zooks thrash.

Ray Yoder took John and Amanda to St. Thomas for a second load of peaches, also summer Rambo apples. That is nice country. There is a settlement of Old Order River brethren around there and they are prosperous.

While we visited Mrs. Effie Brenneman Sunday p.m. a few of the brethren stopped in for a brief visit and I unexpectedly met a man that I had seen about a year ago in a restaurant.

To me it is very interesting to meet people of different denominations, all seem to have good hopes spiritually in trying to serve the Lord.

Horse Power

The Amish have a saying that bears repeating, "A horse re-produces, a tractor produces nothing but debts." Everywhere you look the Amish are making use of the horse. Even among those communities that have turned to limited use of tractors the horse still is the main source of power. The Amish wisely buy older, obsolete tractors at very reasonable prices.

The horse not only provides transportation and power for running farm machinery but it fertilizes fields as well. Contrary to popular belief the Amish are not entirely organic farmers. They will make use of commercial fertilizers when and where necessary. Over the years the Amish have developed an acute farm sense. They introduced some of the most modern techniques in farming long before they were recognized elsewhere. In Europe, before their migration to America, they began experimenting with crop rotation. They were given only

the poorest land to farm, yet they had to make it pay for they always had large families to support and large taxes to pay in order to keep their sons out of the military.

Nowhere in America except in the Amish areas can you see such a bewildering array of horses doing the work they have been bred to do. Although the tractor has moved in more strongly in some areas, it does not seem that it will completely displace the horse. The Jamesport Amishman I spoke of earlier moved from Hutchinson, Kansas, in order to return to the horse farming of his grandfather. I know of at least one non-Amishman in Iowa who claims to be running a profitable farm on nothing but horsepower.

THE BUDGET

WATERLOO, ONT., CAN.
Martins

October 25—It is exceptionally warm and pleasant these days, after having a little snow a week ago. I believe the apples are about all picked now. Abner G. Martin has erected a cider press and apple butter cooking apparatus, which seems to work fine. The last years not many had the chance to get apple butter cooked, as we had to hire a truck to take the apples some 15 miles. With rising costs even the lowly apple butter is selling for 80¢ lb.

George R. Martin's barn is nearing completion, although many small jobs need to be done when it looks finished on the outside. He had a sore leg so that he used crutches for awhile, but is now helping with the work. A horse's hoof had struck him below the knee, while he was getting the horse out of the burning building.

SIX LAKES, MICH.

March 28—Our county is short of funds for road maintenance so they are cutting costs by not running snow plows on secondary roads on weekends. It did not cause much inconvience so far. We had no heavy snow storms this winter. Most of it came a little at a time.

Mose Shetler told me to announce they have a new surrey and a new horse and are ready for visitors. If he brings you by our place, do stop in.

He did mention something about the horse not being broke but it seems to me this should not be much of a problem. Mose is a good horseman and most Belgians are easily trained.

The ground is frozen again the last two mornings.

The ice is on the lakes yet.

Everywhere you look in an Amish community you will find signs of the horse—hitch rails, hardware stores selling horse-blanket pins. In every Amish area you will find sale barns with an ample number of horse sales. In Kalona, Iowa, where I live, they have a horse sale on the first Monday of every month and a number of special sales such as draft horses bring Amish and other buyers from all over the United States.

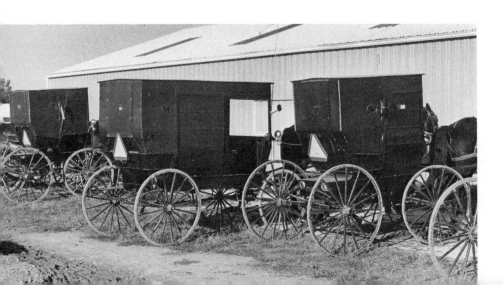

THE BUDGET

CONEWANGO VALLEY, N.Y.

April 13—To Mose Shetler of Mich. (by request of a Budget reader): Don't feel too bad about your Belgium horses. We also have people here in our area that wouldn't want to be caught driving Percheon horses, even after dark in the back 40 acres. But I'd bet a fish dinner they couldn't tell the difference if it wasn't for the horses color.

Blacksmith

What Amish community would be complete without its blacksmith. Kalona has had as many as three, but is now down to one fulltime and one part time. Fulltime blacksmith Willie Shrock (shown on these pages) is kept busy shoeing horses not only of the Amish but also of other horse fanciers from hundreds of miles around. Besides blacksmithing he is also a wheelwright and his son is learning the business. A museum in Chicago recently sent him the wheels from an old fire engine for repair. In addition to the blacksmiths and wheelwrights, there are harness makers, buggy makers, cabinet makers, carpenters and many other sidelines, for most of these Amish workers are fulltime farmers also. We even have one old Amishman who specializes in making grandfather clocks.

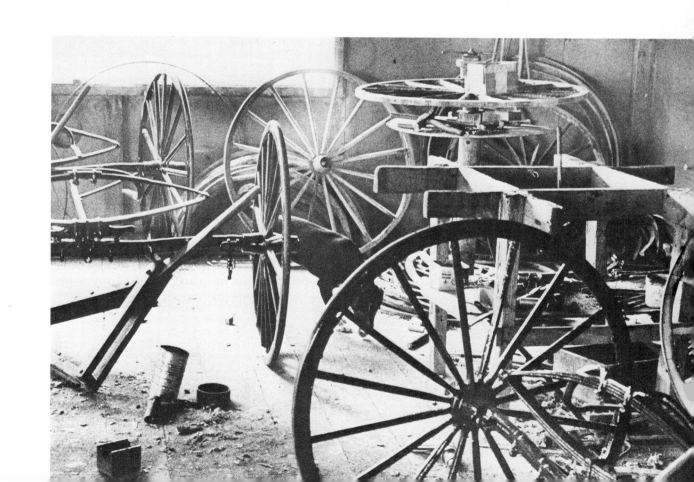

The Land

Next to the Bible and his religion, the land is the most important thing in an Amishman's life. It is the physical manifestation of a gift from God given over to man's safekeeping. He knows that this self-same land may one day be in the hands of his great-great-grand-sons, although others of his sons will have scattered to the four winds seeking yet other good land for their sons and their sons' sons. The Amish have never lost the pioneering spirit and today they are founding new colonies anywhere where there is room to grow.

THE BUDGET

CAAGUAZU, PARAGUAY

Aug. 5—The past week has been quite warm. A shower would be good for garden things.

Since we hear there are more of our people interested in locating in Paraguay a committee from here was chosen to investigate the possibilities of buying land for a new colony. Their investigation led to the conclusion there is yet much land for sale in Paraguay although it is no longer available at the price we paid 8½ years ago. It is never-the-less quite cheap compared to land prices in the States.

Paul and I visited at the John Myers and Porfirio Lopez homes last night then on the way home we saw Clarence Millers were still cooking cane molasses so we stopped in to observe and sample it. Yes, folks are beginning to raise cane in Paraguay too!

They are pressing and cooking for Uria Shetlers today then have some to do for Delbert Bontregers yet.

Lois Eichorn went over to help with it today and perhaps also to share in the trials. Since flowers and things in the bush are frozen the wild bees come out looking for something to eat and cane molasses tastes good. Katie said she only got 6 stings yesterday! Across the road John Masts also have their share of them. Heard say Mahala spent most of one afternoon in the barn instead of in the house out of respect to the bees! They've also been quite thick around the Delbert Bontreger home and perhaps other places as well. I hope Rachel Shetler didn't have any in the house when she entered her kitchen and stood in the molasses! She'd left the kitchen for a little after putting some molasses on the stove to heat a little more.

In case you wonder, her stove is right inside the kitchen door so the molasses did not cover the kitchen floor! In fact, there was only a gallon or so on the floor! Life in Paraguay can be sweet enough at times, verdad?

THE BUDGET

MEYERSDALE, PA.

Thrashing is about done around here. Women folks are kept very busy with canning peaches, tomatoes, beans and corn.

Homers have 3 rows of sweet corn in the field on top of the hill, and this morning while Homers and I were getting a load of corn we saw a doe with her two young ones. They had just come out of the woods and in the hay field and up in the sweet corn. They mostly bite the tops of the ears off.

On Tuesday afternoon a thunderstorm came up. We had .6 tenth inch rain here. Cantaloupes are ripening and are very big this year. Bartlett pears are falling.

ETHRIDGE, TENN.

July 9—Weather is warm. We had a couple of rain showers over the weekend which were greatly appreciated. Blackberry picking is in full swing with blackberries being a good crop. The worst thing about picking blackberries is the jigger bites you receive if you don't put something on to keep them off.

Jiggers are so small a person can't see them with the naked eye, but they feel a lot bigger once they have eaten their way into a person's skin.

The men are putting up second-cutting clover hay now. There is still some oat threshing to do, too. The women are busy putting food into the cellar for next winter.

THE BUDGET

NAPPANEE, IND.

July 24—Quite warm the last while. Men folks are busy thrashing wheat, oats and some barley. Some is yielding real good, while some is not so good.

Blueberries are being picked and are a good crop, also apples are plentiful.

MEYERSDALE, PA.

July 24—Greetings: Yesterday a thundershower went by and missed us, but miles north, they were making hay and it rained a very hard shower seems to go in streaks all summer.

Grain fields look very nice. We are up here in the mountains, but our heavy snow Dec. 1 brought good crops, os it is not all dark.

If we work and try, seems we are provided for, but we must do our part.

I wish we were all able to abide by what the Lord gave us.

APPLE CREEK, OHIO

Aug. 2—The thrashing crews did quite a bit of suffering from the heat wave we've been having the last 3 or 4 days while thrashing oats, which yielded quite bountifully through this immediate area, with some yields going over 90 bu. to the acre and one yield up to 107. Quite a few are wishing for rain. Thrashing is about woundup for the season.

Corn and hay fields could use a lot of rain and to talk about heat the last few mornings the thermometer didn't even drop below 70 degrees and this morning it had not gone as low as 70. In the p.m. it has been near the middle 90's the last several days, with a high humidity and not much air movement.

Some from around here went to the Peoli area to help with a shed raising at Enos R. Yoders, which was to be yesterday.

There are still a few pairs of overshoes here since Mary's funeral, that we don't know where they belong.

THE BUDGET

ASHLAND, OHIO

July 7—Ideal summer weather. Raspberries are on the menu. Seems the fruit crops are bountiful this year. Menfolks are busy cutting and shocking wheat.

Northeast church services are to be at Jesse M. Duckworths and Middle district at John E. Millers on Sunday, July 13th.

Ervin H. Yoders had a mishap while taking Ervin Hersbergers of Kenton visiting last week one morning. The horse they had hitched to the double-seated buggy started kicking, and kicked away the dash-board. The buggy then overturned and the top was pretty well smashed up and one spring broken. Luckily no one was hurt. They had gotten the buggy new about six months ago.

THE BUDGET
RICEVILLE, IOWA

June 29—We are having some nice summer weather with occasional rain. Crops are growing nicely. Haying and cultivating is the work among men folks. Some hay was on the ground over a week on account of rains. Womenfolks are hoeing and starting to can peas which look to be plentiful.

THE BUDGET

CASHTON, WISCONSIN
Monroe & Vernon Counties

August 10—Weatherwise it is getting dry, some pastures are turning brown. Some corn fields are curling up a little over the warmest part of the day, oats are all cut and shocked, threshing is started. Oats are good quality and yield fair, second cutting hay is also being put up and is a fair crop.

Sweet corn and tomatoes are on the menu with muskmelons and watermelons getting close.

Mahlon Gingerich had a close call Sat. when he was coming down the dugway with the mower when his neck yoke broke. He jumped off and the team went on down, his son John, age 10, was going down ahead of him with a team on a hay cart and luckily got out of the way. When the team and mower got to the road the left horse got loose and the right one went over the fence into the pasture and caught the mower on a tree and still had one tug hooked.

No one was hurt, but the right hand horse had a few little gashes on the hind leg, and one mower wheel was broken when it hit a rock.

89

THE BUDGET

WELLSBORO, PA.

July 16—Haying is in full swing. Pepper, our dog enjoys riding on top of the loads from the neighbor's field to our barn, about 3 miles.

GUYS MILLS, PA.

Aug. 22—Women are busy canning corn, tomatoes and pickles. Men are still thrashing when weather permits.

Crist Millers were to Geauga Co., Ohio on Monday taking in a surrey, and bringing back schoolbooks and desks. Mildred Maloney was the driver.

Ervin Miller had a near runaway, on Wednesday when his team and wagon were standing near the thrash machine when it was started up. It scared the horses and they started running. Ervin caught up with the back end of the wagon, and got on. He got the horses under control just before they got to the black top, which was a lucky thing as a car was coming.

AYLMER, ONT., CAN.

Aug. 22—Yesterday we had an all-day rain which should make the pasture grow. Oat threshing is nearly finished. Peaches are ripe and selling for $5.00 a bushel.

The group who went on the blueberry picking excursion did real well. I think forty people went in all from this area, Mt. Elgin and Lakeside, and came back with nearly a ton of blueberries.

Several weeks ago Cephas Kauffman found a fox in the barn one morning. The dog promptly attacked him and after a fight, the fox escaped out the back of the barn. Several days later Philip Wagler found a dead fox along side the road near the gully southeast of Cephas' farm. Since it was assumed the fox was rabid, the dog was taken care of and the incident was forgotten. Several days ago one of the cats started foaming at the mouth and scratched three of the children. Cats are really just as dangerous to spread rabies as dogs and in someways more so.

THE BUDGET

HAZLETON, IOWA

Aug. 21—Very humid after our 1½" rain the past week.

Some corn fields are beyond repair as the rains came too late. Bean fields look nice.

Tomatoes are being canned and some more peaches trucked in or expected this week. Red Havens brought $7.58 to $8.50 bu. brought from Michigan.

Middle East church is to be at Pre. David Yutzys with intended baptismal services for Chester, son of Henry J. Yoder.

Ms. Ed. (Cora) Bontrager is having quiltings here in Iowa. One was last week at Alvin J. Yoders and one on Wednesday at Em. J. Helmuths.

Sam Lehmans are in the Wisconsin area for a couple of days this week.

BLOOMFIELD, IOWA
Davis Co.

July 24—We need a good soaking rain to keep the corn and pastures from drying up. It is about 4 weeks since we've had a good rain and only a few sprinkles since.

Wheat and oats are being combined. Our ring to start thrashing tomorrow. Women folks are working up pickles, tomatoes, and sweet corn.

On July 11 George Gingerichs had a frolic for his relation to work on their house and barn. There was a pick up load from Clark, Mo. and a truck load from Buchanan Co. there, with around 3 doz. men and boys working. Last week they had a frolic for the people around here and the roof was finished on the barn. On Tuesday there was frolic to put an addition on the barn where Eli Yutzy's live.

THE BUDGET

ELKTON, MINNESOTA

Aug. 8—Who will hear our call to come out to Minnesota to help us?

There are five or more farms for sale within a 10 mile radius. The sizes of the farms vary between 200 acres to 425 acres.

The reasons for the farms being sold are that the owners are getting old & their sons are not interested. Speculators bought land when prices were lower and now are selling the farms for profit.

It is a good place for fathers to help their sons, interested in farming, get started. If father doesn't help the son, no one else will. It's a nice quiet place to raise a family. There is room for expansion as sons grow older.

LINWOOD, ONT., CAN.

Aug. 27—No harvesting since last Wednesday. Had a heavy rain last Thursday. Then on Saturday night we had about 5" through the night, and close to an inch since.

Today we are going to try our hand at picking blueberries in Michigan. A charter bus load is going from this area.

HAVEN, KAN.

July 9—The past week has been warmer. Menfolks are busy. Some still have wheat to cut, others are plowing and making second cutting alfalfa.

THE BUDGET

TUNAS, MO.

June 23—Full moon tonight. What a beautiful evening with the pond as smooth as glass, reflecting the full moon. Nothing to disturb the peace and quiet but the croaking of a few frogs and the distant call of a whip-poor-will.

These hot summer days have a way of lowering ones energy. Even the fish aren't biting very well, but the mocking bird doesn't seem to mind a bit. He usually begins his serenade before daylight and continues throughout the day.

Warm as the weather is it's not dry, so there's an abundance of fruit, berries and vegetables to keep the women on the job.

Haying is over. Corn fields look good.

THE BUDGET

SAN MARCOS, HONDURAS

July 28—A freshly washed hilly country side greets us this morning. Upon waking, one hears the ever present sound of the creek. It falls rapidly, among the stones, making a noise of rushing waters. I start fire in the kitchen stove, put on water for oatmeal. After telling mama to have breakfast ready and the children up, I leave to milk the cow taking a glance at the new cement floor in the house. A great improvement that is. The walk to where the cow is is pleasant on this fine morning. I pass the widow's house whose husband died of a wound received when he fell on a stone. She milks 5 cows.

Now I cross the creek on a log thrown across. At this spit it has a fall of about 4 feet. At this crossing, the neighbor women wash their clothes, their corn for tortillos and get water for house use.

Cooking sugar cane is the main work here at present. This is one of the main income crops. Today I went to where they were cooking to get some syrup. It was to far along so they gave me some finished dulce. This is the syrup cooked pretty hard, put up in blocks. That fresh cooked syrup is really good.

The cane is cut by hand with machets. Then it is hauled to the "tropeachy" cane press by oxcart. Here it is unloaded and put on big piles. The oxen also bring in the firewood. A diesel engine makes power for the press. The juice is cooked in a big trough then taken off and put in another trough when its done. From here its put in wooden molds to make the dulce blocks. These are approximately 3x3x4 inches. The syrup is best when about ½ done. The man owning the press goes from place to place.

Mangos are ripe. Also other central American fruits. Also bananas, platinos, Chatos and pineapples. This high, cool area should be good for strawberries, potatoes and most other vegetables. Coffee is also grown here.

Aug. 5—We have about the right amount of rain to make things grow nice. There are not many vegetables grown here but am sure it would be a good vegetable area. Last week one day went to visit a family that live over an hours walk back in the hills. One sees much sugar cane in these hills and here and there is the steam floating upward from the cooking. Makes one think of how we used to cook maple syrup on father's farm in Indiana. Some of these hills have tall straight oak trees. They would sure make a lot of lumber. We arrived at our destination a bit wet as it had rained.

THE BUDGET

ASUNCION, PARAGUAY

Aug. 24—This has been the time of burning extra wood and weeds in fields and pastures. Especially since recent frost has killed some of the growth. We have seen in past years that ranchers make a regular thing out of burning range at this time of the year. It makes room for fresh growth, it kills insects, and if there has been dead wood lying in the pasture it removes some of that. Our interest in burning was more particularly to get rid of wood that was in our way and kill weeds in order to plant corn and mandioca.

We did not want to burn our pasture off at least not completely lest the cows have nothing to eat for a while. But we had to work in order to keep it from happening twice. What did get burned will work for our good I think. However, we do not want to let the rest get burned.

We had cut down growth and old corn stalks on a three-acre piece some weeks back. As the weather continued dry and a frost turned the grass brown conditions were ideal for getting rid of trash without so much work. The first lighting, however, spread into pasture where we have elephant grass and siepre verde. This was not too hard to control. Even though perhaps two and a half hectares (six acres) of pasture were burned we do not need it.

Later we burned a narrow strip along the highway which we intend to use for crops also. We carefully cut a path to control the fire, but the next day it got into the pasture late in the morning and so we had to fight a grass fire for a while.

As of now things seem quite well under control, but we want to check carefully as a dry east wind keeps blowing and embers keep on smouldering. We hope all the smouldering wood is far enough removed from unburned pasture.

The drier weather is quite helpful to us at this time as it facilitates the cleaning up process. Fire is helpful, too but it must be kept under control. For must of the year one has no problem with fire spreading in a pasture.

Somebody mentioned recently about Paraguay being commended in some newspaper or magazine for the fact that divorce is not permitted or not recognized. That by itself sounds good, but the conditions here do not show it to be all good. There are many cases of just "living together" and then evidently when things are not what either one or both want there can be an easy separation. Then there are the separations when there has been a legal marriage, but the wife still has her legal claim on part of the possessions of the husband. There are numerous people who have had an illegitimate birth. If other things were what they should be for the most part, the fact of not having or not recognizing divorce would be fine, too.

The price of soy beans went up nicely and I think most everybody has sold the bulk of what they wished to sell. Philip Riehl has the oil press. Families are using their own cooking oil and the expellers that are left over are an excellent feed for animals.

Down payment has been made on a property for another colony. It is approximately ninety miles from here in the direction of Asuncion. It will be more convenient for the settlers there to get to town and back.

I will need to finish this and some other things and get back to the fires. May the fires be burning constantly upon the altars of the heart. Fire is a great agent for cleaning up for our field. The spiritual fire is a cleansing agent too. "Is not my word like as a fire: saith the Lord . . ."

Amish Homes

The Amish home has a solid no-nonsense feel about it. It is, for the most part, wooden frame and painted white, although some of the strictest Amish do not paint their houses at all. In addition to the main structure there may be a summer kitchen and a wash house, although sometimes one extra room serves as both. Many have porches with the traditional porch swing: a good place to sit on hot summer nights, a place away from the main house for a courting couple to pass the evening talking.

The Amish home is, all in all, rather plain until the Amish woman has had a chance to get to it. Up goes a white picket fence along the road and in front of it long rows of flowers, here and there fruit trees and shrubs and, off to one side, a large vegetable garden, carefully tended with flowers intermixed to give it a look of beauty and peace.

Almost all of the Amish homes I have seen are wooden frame

Amish Acres near Nappanee, Indiana. Although this is a tourist attraction, it gives a good picture of what older Amish homes are like.

THE BUDGET

BLACKVILLE, S.C.

July 10 — Watermelons, cantaloupes, peaches and tomatoes are in full harvest. Pickles, which were a good crop, are about over with.

Again, its the time of year when it's such a busy time for the women. Most all of the canning comes in June and July. It's very warm in the daytime but cools off at night considerably. The gnats are in full swing, also, although we do not have as many here as those who have chicken or cattle farms.

The quilt (upper left) was brought to Iowa in 1857 by the Moses P. Miller family, who migrated from Myersdale, Pa. The quilt, the family bible (below) and other heirlooms are now in the possession of great-granddaughter Marie Herner of Kalona, Ia.

structures. Many of them that have not been taken over from "English" farmers, were built by co-operative effort of the community. With the increasing cost of lumber in recent years the Amish have gone into the demolition business, taking houses apart carefully so that most of the lumber may be re-used. The houses are usually large and rambling, allowing plenty of space for expansion as the family grows.

The center of the Amish home is the kitchen. If the family is among the most strict of the Old Order Amish this may hold the only heat source in winter: the coal and wood burning stove. In my own area of Kalona, many Amish have LP gas heaters but in Canada, even the cooking is still done on wood burning stoves.

Off the kitchen will be a pantry with an ample supply of flour, salt, sugar and other basic ingredients for Amish cooking. Beneath it may be a cellar where the home-rendered lard and other more perishable items are stored.

Amish women spend a great deal of their time cooking, baking and canning. In recent years Amish cookbooks have popped up in almost every Amish region. Along with the traditional Amish recipes like shoofly pie, chow-chow, and German chocolate cake, they eat spaghetti, casseroles and many dishes that are typical of any family.

But the main difference is that they may prepare their own basic ingredients. Egg noodles are quite easily prepared at home and even relatively more difficult things such as cheeses and bologna are included in some Amish recipe books. One Amish woman claimed that she had put up close to a thousand quarts of canned goods by the end of summer.

The Amish have always enjoyed travel and in recent years Amish have become increasingly more mobile by hiring a driver to ferry them from community to community for various activities such as funerals, weddings, frolics, barn raisings. In New Wilmington, Pa., I talked to an Amishman who had only the week before visited the Kalona area. The other day I talked to one of the drivers (who usually

THE BUDGET

BIRD-IN-HAND, PA.

Oct. 9—Communion on Sunday is to be at Eli R. Kings in Bish. Amos E. King district.

On Saturday they intend to ordain a bishop in Jonas King district.

Elmer Millers and Alvin Millers of Iowa, accompanied by Enos Glicks, called here Oct. 4th.

Oct. 5—Emanuel Esh Srs. were here to help dig potatoes. Johns had one potato that weighed 2½ pounds.

Oct. 15—Some of my married children and I intend to go to Mifflin Co. to visit my niece. Rebecca Kauffman, and come home by Brush Valley.

They intend to ordain a bishop in Lower Pequea district, also a minister here. They divided the Brush Valley district.

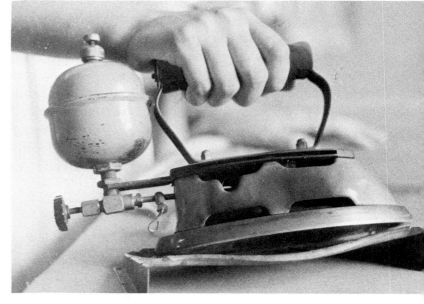

are non-Amish but Amish related with a good command of German) outside a church service in our area. He had brought a number of Amish from Kentucky in a small van. In the past few months he had been in Canada, Minnesota, Michigan, Ohio, Indiana and Pennsylvania. He no more returns home with one group than another is ready to go.

THE BUDGET

MINOR HILL, TENN.

April 3—Temperature again this morning has dropped to 32 degrees. We had some real beautiful weather for a few days. Seems if it's fit to plow, it rains again. We had a lot of rain in the past few months.

On Tuesday night about 12 o'clock we were disturbed by some noise and horn blowing etc. Were surprised to have Emanual Stoltzfus's and their entire family of 13 in all. We gladly bade them enter for the night and soon found out our house wasn't as small as we thought it was.

We were able to plant some garden now, but lettuce, tomatoes, etc. froze. I suppose you people up home are probably ahead of us thus far this year.

The next few days we'll be glad for good cool weather to butcher. Emanuel Stoltzfus and I were to cattle auction the other day and bought a young holstein cow weighing 1230 lbs. We may just try making a few bologna and some hamburger.

The Amish housewife must have a larder sufficiently stocked to take care of a dozen unexpected guests who may be stopping for just a meal or even overnight. She must have enough on hand to feed a large group who come for Sunday church services (and lunch afterward) which rotate among the various Amish homes.

Amish society may be patriarchal but an Amish woman has charge of the home. She must co-ordinate dozens of minor and major activities to keep the home running smoothly. When strawberries are coming in, so many days must be allotted to picking, cleaning and

REBERSBURG, PA.

Sept. 1—Tomatoes are about ready to pick and third cutting hay is a good crop. We had over 2 inches of rain this week.

Melvin Zook, Eli Beiler, the writer and wife attended a frolic at Amos Eshs in Leb. Co. Tuesday.

Abner Kings have a little boy born Wed., Aug. 28 named Andy. This makes 10 children for Abbies, 6 boys and 4 girls.

Amos, 8 yr. old son of Sam J. Stoltzfuses, broke his left arm again. This is the third time in several years. Amos is left handed.

preserving—either by making jellies and jams, canning or freezing.

Long before re-cycling became a household word, the Amish woman was re-cycling all manner of store bought food jars into home canning use. They also keep a watchful eye out at auctions to buy used canning jars. At times you can find jars that have been in use 40 to 50 years.

Off the kitchen usually is a parlor. Here beaus are entertained by eligible daughters while the family discreetly finds chores in other parts of the house; visiting neighbors are entertained during the winter months and women gather for sewing bees in the months before the daughter's wedding. Friends and relatives gather to fill her hope chest with embroidered pillow cases, sheets and coverlets and handsomely made quilts. The first sign that the newly married daughter will be adding a new member to the family brings another round of sewing

THE BUDGET

JACKSON CENTER, PA.

June 5—We are having rain lately and had a hard thunderstorm during the night.

May 24—Rudy Troyers had a frolic to work on their barn siding and washhouse. Around 25 men attended. The women quilted. Jonas A. Miller had a frolic the same day to work on his barn.

crib quilts, blankets and new dresses and other clothes for the infant. Even the boys wear dresses in the first year of life to facilitate diaper changes in a world where the zipper is classed as "too worldly". This is also a time for patching up anything that has survived being handed down from younger brothers and sisters. If the item is too much in tatters it can become part of a rag rug to keep babies' feet off cold winter floors.

Even the simple home tasks such as doing washing and ironing require more effort on the part of Amish women. If they are among

THE BUDGET

HALFWAY, MO.
(Buffalo Area)

July 23—Warm, busy summer days. Women folks are snowed under with corn, blackberries, pickles and now peaches. Monday the ladies got together and had over a hundred quarts corn in the freezer by 11 o'clock in the forenoon. Today over 300 qts. were put up at Owen Kropfs again for different people.

the most modern of the Old Order group they may have a gasoline operated motor on their washing machine; if not, they may depend on the hand operated variety which is still be manufactured and requires a good set of back muscles.

Ironing without electricity might seem a grueling task, but a few inventions which came along a hundred or so years ago have come into use. One is the kerosene powered iron which is pictured on these pages. It is lighted and pressurized in much the same manner as modern camping lanterns. What you get instead of light is a nice hot iron. But then, Amish clothes are generally made from good strong long-lasting fabrics.

Lighting in the Amish home is almost universally provided by the kerosene lamp, although, most today use the kind with the pressurized system that gives as much light as the normal electric bulb.

The Amish home is never cluttered, since only the necessities are allowed. For example, shades but not curtains. However, the enterprising Amish housewives have found loopholes in Amish philosophy and the word useful has been stretched to fit quite a number of items. A postcard of a beautiful vacation scene sent by a friend or relative becomes a wall decoration—after all it served a purpose. Intricately painted china plates are displayed in China cabinets but are also ready for use by extra guests. The Amish make it a practice to pick up all the free calendars available in the town and an

especially pleasing scene may hang on the wall years beyond its usefulness. Amish women using their skill with a needle and thread have created all manner of decorative and useful items as well as sew the clothing for all the family.

The Amish house contains no more store bought items than absolutely necessary. In years past there were even Amish cobblers, but most hats and shoes are now store bought.

THE BUDGET

LAUREL HILL, PA

April 13—It is rather late to have frost in the early morning hours.

But not at the place where the man and wife had an argument while getting out of bed. She said, she believes there is a frost this morning, the husband didn't think so and stepped out unto the porch roof to investigate and slid down over. The wife was right they did have a frost.

Family Life

THE BUDGET

MIFFLINTOWN, PA.
(Juniata Co.)

August 22—Is still rather dry here. Oats are mostly all thrashed or combined. Farmers are plowing and getting ready to fill silo. Womenfolks are busy filling jars with peaches, applesauce, tomatoes, lima beans and vegetable soup, etc. for use. Peaches are selling for around $6.00-$7.50 per bushel. Apples around 4-5 dollars per bushel. They are plentiful but quite small due to dry weather.

The community was shocked to hear of the tragic accident and death of Levi H. Peachey, age 39, on Monday p.m. August 18. He was employed by William Peoples as hired man on the farm. Nobody really knows how it happened as he was alone at the time but they think he drove out over the edge too far when turning and the tractor toppled down over the 10 ft. bank onto the road, pinning him underneath. Part of his body was crushed which probably killed him instantly, and his face, arms and chest were badly scalded from hot water from the radiator. He will be greatly missed in the home, the community and as a song leader in church.

112

Today when we speak of family in America we visualize a mother and father, two children and somewhere off in the background, perhaps a thousand miles away one or two pairs of grandparents. We see that family jumping into the car or perhaps one of the new motor homes and vacationing at the other end of America. In short, today's average American family is small and mobile.

When the Amish speak of family it is mother and father, five, six, seven—even 14 children; a grandfather and grandmother living in the same house, and perhaps even a great grandfather or grandmother. It is a host of aunts and uncles, first cousins and second cousins, and hundreds of blood kindred.

A copy of the *Bloody Theatre* of *Martyrs' Mirror* is to be found in nearly every home and through it has been burned into the minds of each and every member of that family that they are a people set apart,

a people who must stand against the encroachments of the modern world in the same way their ancestors stood against the Martyr's fire. Every family has, besides the *Martyrs' Mirror,* an ancient German family Bible in which the births, weddings and deaths in a family may have been recorded for over a century. Next to to those are the intricate genealogical records that bespeak a much stronger attachment to the past than to the present. It is an awareness on the part of every Amish man, woman, and child of an ancestoral line going back to Jacob Hostetler, who came to America in the early 1700s, or Daniel Guengrich, who came later, or even back to origins in Switzerland.

The Amish family is the sum and total of all who went before. From booklets, pamphlets, mimeographed sheets and even large bound books come autobiographical sketches of early settling, reminiscents

of the first years in a new community. In this way discoveries and triumphs as well as failures can be shared with all members of the "family".

In a way this provides remarkable security for all family members. A young boy learns as soon as he is able what his role will be in life. There are no decisions about whether to be a fireman or doctor; he is to be a farmer. For a young girl it is motherhood and being a good farm wife.

The family is both a brotherhood and a learning institute in much the same manner a vocational school might be. Every one is instructed in his or her job then through practice learns to do it in the best possible way. If they have mastered one task then another, bigger one is given them. In this way the Amish boy steps behind the plow to spell his father and in later years he will be doing the major part of the

THE BUDGET

BARNETT, MO.

July 2—We are having warm summer weather. Only rain was a few sprinkles. Some are eating roastin' ears and selling them for one dollar a doz. String beans are plentiful. About everybody seems to have plenty of that kind of vegetables. Tomatoes are not quite ripe yet.

Wild plums, gooseberries and dew berries are plentiful. While we went picking these one day last week we frightened a buck out of the bushes on our land.

CENTREVILLE, MICH.

Jan. 17—Mrs. Tobe Yoder has 2 Tingley boots for the same foot for her 2 year old son. They somehow got mixed up here at our place in church. It's easy to get a Tingley boot on the wrong foot, but if one remembers the buttons go on the outside part of the leg it's easy to see.

heavy farm work as his father more and more takes over a supervisory role. In the same way the Amish girl begins to take over her mother's chores so that she may devote her time to more intricate details as well as taking care of an increasing number of younger brothers and sisters.

If the Amish work together they also play together. Annual school picnics, family re-unions or just plain after Sunday service visiting are all part of the shared pleasures of life.

The Amish family is very much like the big family of the last century—full of tradition and ceremony, full of expectations, full of old-fashioned fun like taffy pulls and most importantly full of old-fashioned honest work.

In the winter you can see them all gathering round the kitchen stove, eating fresh popcorn while mother knits and children draw, read or play simple games, while father works to mend a harness. Father may take time out to read from the German Bible to all. The

younger children may practice their German words. Then, perhaps, they will discuss the meaning of the stories and words from the book.

One of the strongest morals an Amish father teaches is non-aggression and non-competition. Wars are started by those who want to win something from another. The Amish teach their children that winning is not the important thing, it is the enjoyment of the game. In the same way they work with nature, not against it. In this way they live in peace and brotherhood with both man and nature—and in respecting both they have prospered—despite their non-progressive ways.

America has always been touted as the great melting pot, yet on closer examination it is anything but that. You can put a MacDonald's hamburger stand on every main street in America but that will not make all towns alike. This is even true with the Amish. You may think of them as just one single group, but there are many minor regional differences. Two of the most fascinating and least known are the yellow and white buggy Amish of Kishcoquillas Valley, Mifflin Co. Pennsylvania.

The valley was settled around 1790 and the Amish who live there look as if they had stepped right out of the Revolutionary War period. The yellow buggy group are most distinguished by the yellow-painted buggy and their penchant for serving bean soup after church services. The white buggy Amish are radically different from any other Amish group. They considered the windmill, the symbol of almost every Amish farm today, "too worldly" when it came into use over 100 years ago. Likewise, the Amish women do not wear the bonnets that are today a symbol of Amish womanhood.

The men wear their hair to shoulder length with bangs and a small widebrimmed hat that perches atop their head much in the manner of the early Pilgrims. They wear only white shirts and no suspenders or belts (most Amish can be identified by their use of suspenders). The women wear ankle-length dresses, the longest of any Amish group, and a black kerchief is used to cover the white prayer cap. (See in the color section the typical little Amish girl compared with one from Kishcoquillas Valley.)

Their houses, too, are survivors of another era—unpainted and without eaves. This group of Amish is by far the most reluctant to be photographed, so I had to content myself with working at a distance. But I felt they deserved particular notice for they demonstrate how the past can survive in the "nooks and crannies" of this great land.

Social Life

Amish social life revolves around faith, and their faith embodies in it all that they may say and do with their lives. It is said that one of the reasons that the Amish did not accept electricity was that it required a man to work on Sunday. Sunday is very much the Lord's day among both the Amish and Mennonites.

If you chance through Amish country on a Sunday you may see them gathered around an Amish home for church services. As many as 40 buggies may be in the yard. Church services are held bi-weekly with many Amish areas having a shorter Sunday school service on alternate Sundays. In my own area of Kalona, two different church districts have alternated in the use of one small white frame building for their Sunday school. It has been known locally for years as "Dutch College."

The Amish ministers have no formal church training. In fact, every Amishman is expected to be ready to accept the call from God if it comes to him. With the death of the old minister a new one must be chosen by lot. The Bibles of all eligible men in the church district are

placed on a table with a marker in only one. Then, the men draw lots and the one that receives the Bible with the marker becomes the new minister serving for life or until ill health does not allow him to carry on. So, each man must work hard throughout his life mastering High German Bible just in case he is chosen.

Church services in the home involve a lot of advance preparation, everything must be spick and span, and food must be prepared for lunch after services. Where Sunday services are to be held is easily identified by the bench wagon parked near the house. This bench wagon looks much like an old-fashioned hearse and is used to transport the long wooden backless benches that are the main seats. Only the elderly or visitors are provided with more comfortable seating.

The service begins with a hymn from the *Ausbund,* one of the oldest Protestant hymn books. A leader begins the singing and others join in. No musical instruments are allowed either in service or in general. The harmonica seems to be "winked at" in most communities and

THE BUDGET

CROCKET, KY.

Jan. 13—We are having an unusual amount of snow. It came down thick and fast, measuring at least 8½ inches. It took a little more effort to get to church but not that anyone couldn't get there because of it.

Last evening was the deacon ordination in which Clinton Amstutz and Elam Weavers shared the lot. Clinton Amstutz is the one chosen of God for the deacon work.

THE BUDGET

MIDDLEFIELD, OHIO

April 19—Much needed showers yesterday and last night. We have had a cool north wind for all the month of April, or so it seemed. The cold nights along with the sun in the day time really dried the ground out. Quite a bit of oats were sowed and a lot of plowing has been done. The grass has not grown much at all.

Council meeting was held at our home last Sunday. Visitors were Bishop Dan N. Gingerich. Communion services are planned for Sunday the 27th at Freeman Gingerichs with plans to ordain a minister as our Bishop Wm. Gingerich is getting up in years. He will be 78 years old this fall, but still gets around good and still works around the home farm where their son Simon lives. Will was born on this farm and has lived there all his life.

cornfield there are two paths, each about 5 ft. wide by 75 ft. long, where the corn is laid flat as if the wind was extra strong there, too.

It sets a mind to thinking; this was just a small storm compared to real tornadoes and hurricanes that have destroyed many lives, homes, etc. in other areas. How very lucky and thankful we are.

Helful hint: To get the best taste out of your canned peaches, add Fruit Fresh, (ascorbic acid or vitamin C) and Karo to your syrup when canning them. Also, if you add bay leaves to your vegetable soup, it'll turn out even better.

And while we're on the subject of canning, those of you who don't should start saving your Ball jar lids and use them a second time. With Kerr, it's probably not possible. It was reported a local store got in two semi-loads of lids, which is an unbelievable amount. But if people would only buy as needed and not try to stock up for the next ten years, maybe the stores wouldn't be so afraid to put them on the shelves for those who truly need them. It's gotten so that whenever someone sees lids, it's gettem, without a thought to needing them or not. So it's really the peoples own fault that no more are available. If I've ruffled a few feathers, so be it.

THE BUDGET

MIDDLEFIELD, OHIO
Mespo-Middlefield Area

The storm of storms broke Sunday just as some of the crowd was finished eating (in church) and so the men had to stay in the basement for awhile longer and didn't see how bad it really was. Dave Detweiler's two-seater tipped over and a post was broken, however, his son said the buggy wasn't worth more than $30 to start with! Another buggy also blew over on its side and was righted again after the storm abated.

The creek behind Enos's house was gushing by like the Falls of Niagara and it had been completely dry beforehand. A big tree or part of one blew over in Atlee Wengerd's yard, falling against the house, but no damage was apparant unless the windows were broken. They weren't home, of course, which is just as well because they would probably have had heart failure!

What looked like the damage of a small tornado or whirlwind of sorts in our sweet corn and neighboring field of corn was amazing. Where our neighbor's sweet corn is still standing tall and straight, ours is flat except for a few stalks that apparently weren't in the twister's path. In the

THE BUDGET

WATERLOO, ONT. CAN.
7-26

Douglas Lehman's have moved to Waterloo after being in the house where Oscar Weber's moved out over a year ago. Lehman's had been there almost a year and attended our church services regularly until this Spring when the husband decided the plain way is too narrow for him. They had come from Niagara Falls after being interested in one way of life, which to her would still be dear, but to be submissive to her husband she has gone back to town with him and the children.

many a teenage boy or girl may have one. When I asked one of them what he played, he replied hymns. Naturally, with no radio or other means of hearing new tunes they have to depend on old standbys.

The services are long ones and the main sermon may last longer than an hour, interspaced with readings from scriptures and silent prayer. In all, it may run to over three hours. A certain amount of fortitude is required to last that long. "Woe to them that are at ease in Zion . . . (Amos 6:1)". A great deal of allowances are made for younger children who may wander about during the service or stop for cookies or crackers and milk.

It is very much a patriarchal society and the women are seated separately from the men. After the services, lunch begins in a series of shifts. The oldest men first, then the younger and finally the women and children. Menus vary from place to place but are usually kept simple to discourage competition among the various housewives in whose homes the services are held. Coffee, milk, cheese, bread, apple

butter, peanut butter, pickles, perhaps even some cold cuts, usually suffice.

After lunch they all may sit around the lawn visiting for an hour or so or be off down the road to visit friends or relatives. There is almost always a new baby to see and admire or an old person to visit. But, by evening they must return home for there are certain farm chores that must be done, even on Sunday. I knew one Amish girl who from the age of eleven to twenty-one milked the cows morning and night, with only a few days off during all the time, for her brothers considered the milking woman's work and the mother was too busy most of the time to take over yet another chore.

Although major church services are held only every other week, the church influence is carried over into even the fun activities. Young people get to know each other when they gather for "Singing" and the songs, of course, come from the *Ausbund*. Young people are not official members of the church until they are baptized, usually around the age of 16, although it is possible to put it off for two years, but not without increasing pressure from family and other church members.

It is usually at this point that the break with the old way of Amish

WATERLOO, ONT., CAN.
Martins

October 11—We are enjoying lovely autumn weather. Leaves are beginning to fall.

The men in this district are kept busy helping at George Martins new barn, which is well under way, hoping to have a raising in the very near future. This is an exciting time for the women also, as tables are spread in our manner and everyone sits down to a warm meal. On such a day one can expect between 200 and 300 people, men and women.

I forgot to mention that George Martin, whose barn burned down, was hurt while getting his horses out at the time of the fire. The horse's shoe struck him on the front of his leg below the knee, so he is on crutches. Their address is West Montrose, R.R.2, Ont.

THE BUDGET

BELLEVILLE, PA.

Jan. 15—David C. Peachy farm sale was held yesterday with a large, shivering crowd from many nearby Amish communities. If this sale is a pattern of the farm sales to come this spring, good horse drawn machinery will be higher. Horses average and cows lower. The high cow brought $825. Most selling in the $400 to $500 range, but some less. He had 2 teams that brought $1000 or better a team.

faith occurs. The young man or woman may decide to join the Beachy church (or "Rubber Dutch") as they permit the use of cars, modern tractors, electricity and telephones, although the dress is almost identical to the other group.

The Amish in my area claim they lose only one in ten to more liberal groups or to the outside world, but I would put it as high as three in ten. But with all this, the Old Order Amish are still growing faster than the general population.

Technically, if these young people fail to join and go out into the world, they are to be placed under a ban or Meidung. This means they are to be shunned by friends and family. In actual fact, this shunning is far from totally enforced today.

Outside of the church related activities such as funerals and weddings, a large part of the other social activities are work related. There are working bees of various kinds from harvest time husking bees to wood cutting bees. A sawing bee was held recently in our area to prepare enough fuel to see a recently widowed woman through the winter. There is an old German proverb that fits the Amish perfectly: "Work makes life sweet." When there is not work, there are the family reunions, or the combination visit and barn raising that may take the Iowa Amish to Pennsylvania or vice versa.

There are other simple pleasures. A good country auction can draw the Amish from miles around. For here is a chance to combine both business and pleasure. Here the Amish can visit with others from nearby church groups and can also look for a bargain. If it is an Amish farm, a much needed piece of horse drawn farm equipment may come up for bid. Unfortunately, the Amish today must compete with the antique dealer for many items they use daily and the rest of the world collects.

The Amish also are very much a part of the small farming communities. Although most of the town businesses are run by non-Amish the very livelihood of the community frequently depends on the horse and buggy trade. The Amish, in turn, need all the shops that the town can provide. Most Amish farms are grouped within three to seven miles of such a town since the horse and buggy or wagon are not the most efficient means of transportation. A three mile drive takes about half an hour at a normal clip, so the Amish generally prefer to come in for shopping early on Saturday morning as did the farmers of old. Anyone wanting to visit an Amish area can be fairly certain that early Saturday morning will find a lot of buggies on the road headed to and from town.

Although the Amish do hire cars and drivers to take them to the bigger cities if they need to consult with a medical specialist or need some equipment and service which is just not available in the small town, they still, by and large, stay as much out of this modern world as they can. I remember one Amishman asking me after seeing Connecticut license plates on my van: "Where's Connecticut—over next to Ohio?" I remember a young Amish boy of about nine or ten in Kalona asking me: "What's Iowa City like?" It is eighteen miles from Kalona and he had never seen it. He also had never seen a movie and watched only a few hours of television because he had visited non-Amish neighbors.

Amish life is a form of a circle with all eyes looking inward. Excursions into the outside world are made grudgingly only when necessary.

The Budget; A Weekly Newspaper Serving the Sugarcreek Area and Amish-Mennonite Communities throughout the Americas—so reads the masthead of this newspaper edited by Sylvester R. Miller that ties together the Amish of all the communities in the Americas. Its design is a simple one. Each week it carries a series of letters from Apple Creek, Ohio, to Auscension, Paraguay, from correspondents who inform you of the weather, the crops, who visited and who was born and who died: essentially every facet of their lives in that area.

Children

"Lo, children are an heritage of the Lord: and the fruit of the womb is his reward. (Psalms 127:3)"

An Amish home is never complete without a stairstep line of little children. Each in his or her turn must learn to work as part of the family team. The youngest child may be given the task of feeding the chickens and as he grows older perhaps raising his own geese. By the time boys are nine or ten they have ridden with their fathers behind the horse teams plowing and planting. They may already be in charge of bringing him the alternate team needed to complete the plowing. Within a short time the son will be spelling his father on the simpler tasks.

Every child, whether boy or girl, must learn to handle horses, for they are the means of transportation and livelihood. Young children may be given a pony which they learn to feed and care for, then, next,

a pony cart to hitch to the pony so they can practice driving. Soon they may be asked to run errands to nearby farms.

Young children are brought up to imitate and emulate their parents, even from the time they are finally out of diapers they are dressed much like miniature adults, especially on special occasions like church or a Saturday visit to town.

Those Saturday visits are often a special treat for the children. They provide sights and sounds far different from what they are accustomed to and father may give them a dime to spend on candy. If they should get a chance to go along to a nearby big city with their parents they are much like children taken to a circus. A shopping center provides them with a wealth of new experiences.

THE BUDGET

SPENCER, WIS.

July 4—Silo filling and haymaking are in full swing. Some early planted corn is over knee high. Early planted sweet corn is coning into tassels. Strawberries are a good crop this year. Peas are blooming and starting to fill out.

An ice-cream supper was held at the Coblentz home last night with a game or so of volley ball.

School is only a little over a month away and no teacher has been found yet. Anyone interested?

THE BUDGET

KENSINGTON, OHIO
Carols from Carroll

October 28—Another beautiful week has gone by with Saturday and Sunday being clear and sunny.

We were reminded the time of HALLOWEEN IS AT HAND. When Luke took the visiting boys to John Mullets for the night, he found at the end of our lane the iron gate closed with a new chain and locked with a new lock and a note attached which read:
"We've set you up for a nice little hunt,
And you must go looking
To find what you want.
You must go find
The key it's true,
But to help you out
Here's a clue.
Beside the sixth fence post (west)
If you don't go wrong
You'll find something there

To help you along."
When he got to the fence post he found this note:
"We know that you're clever
Sly as a fox,
So now go look
In your mailbox."
Going to the mailbox he found this note along with the key to the lock and eight nice cup cakes.
"Now that it's over,
Admit you had fun,
You got a reward
For your little run.
Into your day
We've added some spice,
Now aren't you glad
We've done something nice?"
Now I'm wondering who played this trick.
If I knew I'd send them this note.
"Open the gate
Come right on in
We've got some good cupcakes
They won't cost you a thing."

143

From "Portrait of Iowa"

THE BUDGET

TOWNVILLE, PA.

Jan. 19—Sunshine, rain and snow with lots of wind. Sunday school was at Mose Shrocks; also hymn singing for young folks this evening.

THE BUDGET

TUNIS, MO.

Sept. 6—The weather is warm and dry again.

Visitors in church, Edna Martin from Lanc. Co., Pa.

Other visitors to arrive here for a few weeks stay are Mr. and Mrs. Frank Stauffer and Charlotte Martin from Ephrata, Pa. and Thomas Wenger from St. Marys, Md.

Melton Prairie school house is finished and school started on Tues, the 9th of Sept. with about 32 pupils and Diane and Kevin Wenger as teachers.

THE BUDGET

BARNETT, MO.

Jan. 16—We played the game of basketball at school one day as indicated in our English books. Pick 2 teams and give individual verbs to the pupils one at a time. See if they can make a sentence with that verb. If they can, they score a basket for their team. If not, the person has to go up and write a sentence on the blackboard. But it may not be counted as a score.

The Amish man does not have a large family so that they may go out into the world, be educated and move away. Since his farm is unmechanized, he needs all the efficient workers he can get. Although this may seem like a life of constant drudgery it is far from it. Anyone who visits an Amish farm will see that the children have plenty of time between chores for games. For the boys, baseball is the most important single game, played avidly from spring to winter. Winter brings its own special pleasures: ice skating, sledding, snow ball fights, and whatever else a young mind can devise. Girls play jump rope, hide and seek, and other games, all to German lyrics, for it is often not until they begin going to school that they will learn any English.

A common fallacy about Amish children is that they are little angels. Just because they look like wide-eyed innocents does not mean they always behave that way. An Amish child is less inclined to get into major trouble, probably because his home is one of the most stable to be found anywhere in the world. Divorce and separation are virtually unknown. And, a child never lacks for attention either from parents or numerous brothers, sisters, aunts, uncles, cousins. He never lacks for food or clothing, although homegrown and handmade. He knows that throughout his Amish life he can travel anywhere there are Amish and be assured of food and a place to sleep without mention of money.

THE BUDGET

MOUNTAIN VIEW, MO.

March 24—Sunday school at the Mary Hochsteder home.

I forgot to mention the upset that Mary Hochstedler and the girls had last Sunday, The reach poles broke right behind the fifth wheel, and Black Jack, the faithful old horse, trotted on down the road with the shafts and front axle. There were a few scratches and bruises but nothing serious. Jr. Hatfield, our neighbor, noticed the horse coming down the road and stopped him.

On our recent trip I noticed that the desire for farming is still present in many of young people. But for a great many of the younger ones farm life is a thing of the distant past and no thought is given to attempting anything other than day labor.

When I was a boy, the youngsters who went to school with me wore thin, faded clothes and carried a meager lunch. We were all poor but we didn't know it, and thought nothing of it. Our parents didn't think of leaving the farm for something better, because there was nothing better. With the industrial boom brought on by World War II this changed.

Life on the farm has always been a good life, but the rewards are often slow in coming. This process of slow acquisition is not compatible with today's theory that we have the right to expect the same luxuries and benefits that those outside the farming circles indulge in. The young man wanting to start farming today is often the victim of improper instruction. He expects to start on the same level that his father quit at. He has been left with the impression that he should be enjoying the blessings which God in truth has reserved for the aged to enjoy after many years of hard labor.

Many young people who quit the farm could succeed if they were not in such a hurry to acquire their goals. I recently read an account of a family whose hardships on the farm were capped by the loss of their farm home. Is is said the father was left with only his overalls and thirty-five cents. The banker refused him a loan, but they stuck with it and finally pulled through. It is said that many years later this man's farming assets totaled more than those of the bank which refused him the loan. To start farming today without financial help from some interest individual requires patience and spiritual insight as well as material management.

It is God's plan that the young should earn their bread by the sweat of the brow. And the old enjoy the fruits of a life well spent. But too often our thoughts are in line with the thinking of the world and not with the teachings and ways of God. Too often our thoughts are expressed by the words of Thomas Carlyle who said, "The greatest grievance I have with God is that I am in a hurry and he is not."

Although the Amish believe that idle hands and idle minds are the devil's workshop, there is still enough time left over for a few pranks. In my area we had a raft of mailboxes being blown up with firecrackers and more than one outhouse has been turned over. Amish children are capable of playing practical jokes on fellow children and even parents, sometimes to the detriment of their posteriors.

Although the Amish child may not have much in the way of personal possessions, he has a great deal of love and companionship and the certainty that a large family and his church will always stand by him as long as he stands by the faith.

THE BUDGET

WINDSOR, MISSOURI

Aug. 6—We had a refreshing ½" of rain on Sat. eve., but it quit before the cracks in the ground were filled. Things cooled off considerably though.

Min. Henry Masts and Eli M. B. Millers from Holmesville, Ohio arrived here Sat. eve. to look over their future homes. They attended church services at Eldon Beachys Sunday.

With their help we chose a building site for a schoolhouse on Henry's farm and plans are being made to build a new building this summer. We had hoped to find a used building which could be moved, but looked in vain. We even went to Green Ridge and looked at the schoolhouse which the Amish had build about 20 years ago in hopes of moving it, only to find it wasn't available. Since there are so few here to build a new building, we can't plan on finishing in time for school to start so will probably use a room in Henry's house until the schoolhouse is ready.

THE BUDGET

GUTHRIE, KENTUCKY

Jan. 10—Lots of people were missing Sunday school on Sunday, mostly due to flu and chicken pox which are both making the rounds.

153

School

School for the Amish harkens back to another era, to a time when the three R's were considered enough. They believe that too much education causes their children to become "too worldly" desiring all the materialistic things they see around them.

As in almost all else, their schools are of another century. The one room little red school house with its pot bellied wood stove and its eight grades together is still the mainstay of the Amish educational system.

For many years the Amish had been content to leave the education to the general public school system, as long as that system continued to maintain one room country schools, but when consolidation and bussing began the Amish began building their own one room school houses, modernized at times with LP gas heaters and modern lanterns.

In recent years the Amish also founded Pathway Publishers to produce text books and related materials for Amish school use. In keeping with the old order way the presses are all hydraulic and need no electricity. Much of the books, magazines and pamphlets it published are hand assembled by volunteer help.

When it was proposed that a local group of Amish children be transported to the local community school where they would be taught in a separate room, one Amish father replied: "We want our children country-minded, not city-minded."

THE BUDGET

BLOOMFIELD, IOWA
Davis Co.

November 1—After a rather dry fall it has been raining the last few days and we are doing our fall plowing.

We have our corn all picked but the soybeans are still out in the field.

Last Sat. morning at 9:00 the annual Iowa Amish school meeting got under way here at the Pleasant View School. There were 18 teachers and around 60 board members and other interested people here from Milton, Kalona and Hazleton, Iowa.

For a number of years Amish fathers had to disobey the law in order to educate their children as they wished. The law said only someone with a college education and state teaching certificate could be allowed to teach. The Amish teachers, for the most part had no more than eight grades of official education. In talking with Amish teachers I found that many had taken correspondence courses and in at least one instance had attended university courses in education, although not for official credit.

A recent U.S. Supreme Court decision in the case of the State of Wisconsin vs. Jonas Yoder et al., put an end once and for all to the problem by ruling that the Amish had the right to educate their own children, since their education was important to their life style. Since

then new Amish one room schoolhouses have been appearing in all the Amish areas. These schools are built with the co-operative efforts of the whole Amish community. Land is donated along with lumber and all the skills necessary to erect the school. If other communities could depend on such widespread co-operation among all its members, perhaps we could erect new schools without the necessity of floating million dollar bond issues and raising property taxes.

A recognized expert on Amish culture and religion, John A. Hostetler, professor of anthropology and sociology, (born an Amishman in the Kalona area) states in his study, *Children in Amish Society:* "Something has been seriously wrong with our public policy and the education of our minority groups. At issue was not learning the basic skills but basic values."

He went on to point out that Amish pupils scored higher than other pupils in rural public schools in the basic skills: arithmetic, spelling and word usage. That the Amish have "schools without walls" at home where the children received vocational training in farm and domestic tasks required by their culture. Those who wish to leave are readily assimilated into larger society, as Hostetler himself is a case in point. In fact, he had written me many years ago that he well could have been one of the boys in my "Amish Boys Running" photo that appears at the beginning of this book.

THE BUDGET

MOUNT FOREST, ONT., CAN.

Jan. 30—Yesterday we had enough rain to make the roads icy. There was no school. We had enough snow, though, that there still is sleighing.

The past week, we all had the flu around here.

Amsey Bearingers had a girl's quilting on Tuesday.

To the Versailles scribe: Don't worry about the sleep you lost over your lard. If you had a 48 gallon kettle almost full with lard, at the present price, you must have about two hundred dollars worth of lard. Think of all the popcorn you can make!

THE BUDGET

KALONA, IOWA

April 10—Spring does not seem to be here yet. We are having lots of cloudy weather and also a drizzling rain on Tuesday. No oats sown yet.

On Monday, there was a frolic to make wood, at Eldon Nisleys for both Eldons and Daniel Masts. Eldon had the misfortune of getting his fingers in the gears of a mixer and the tips of the two middle fingers of his right hand were taken off. He is expecting one of his brothers of Indiana here by tomorrow, to help him with his work.

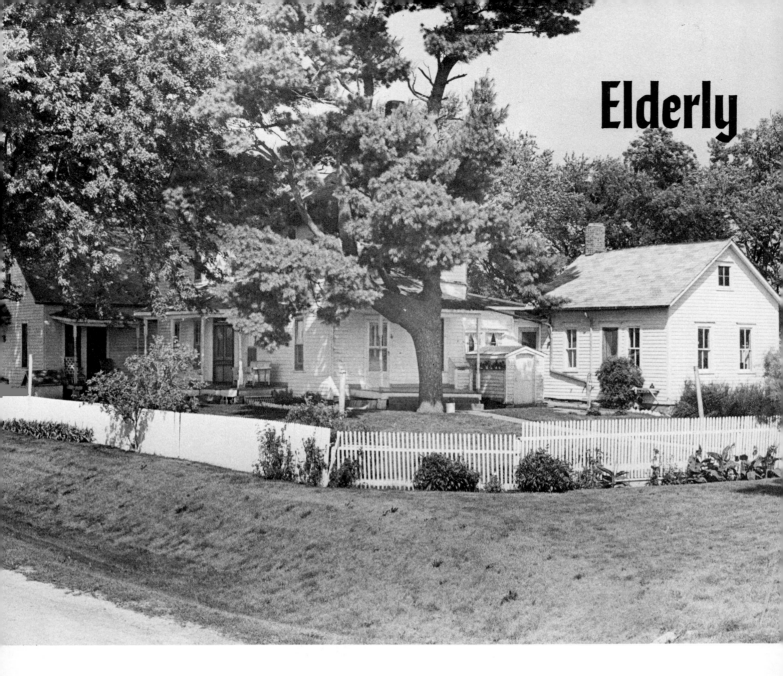

Even the end of their lives seems to come more softly to the Amish. An Amish old age home is a "grandpa" house (Grosdaadi Haus) attached to the main house when the old couple moves to let the last married son or daughter take over the elders' farm responsibilities.

Control of the farm is usually relinquished gradually as the young couple demonstrate their ability to manage a farm. So for neither parents nor children is there an abrupt changing of roles, but a gradual transition. The old people maintain their independence, for the grandpa house is a separate little home of its own connected by a breezeway to the main house. The old couple always have a horse and buggy so that they may go where they choose without depending on the young people.

By the time an Amishman reaches 60 he has usually accumulated enough savings for a satisfactory retirement. The Amish do not believe in Social Security or any other forms of assistance. They are

THE BUDGET

SALEM, IND.

July 16—Having the privilege of getting acquainted with the many different kinds of woods in the mill yard, we came across some red elm. The inner bark is an old-fashioned remedy which has many uses. It is highly nourishing and very soothing and healing wherever it is used.

Slippery elm will stay on an ulcerated and cancerous stomach where nothing else will. It is very nourishing and in case of famine a person could live for some time on the inner slippery elm bark. It is known as one of the most effective ingredients for poultices. It will roll up the mucous material troubling the patient and pass it down through the intestines. It cleans, heals and strengthens. It makes good food for children when mixed with soy bean milk. To make the tea use a heaping tablespoon to a pint of boiling water. Let soak one hour, then simmer a few minutes. Strain and use. It is well to soak and simmer twice as the full virtue does not usually come out the first time. More could be said of its healing abilities and if interested, write.

THE BUDGET

STUARTS DRAFT, VA.

Jan. 10—The talk of the town this week has centered on the "well-known" Dr. Rheims from the Blue Ridge Lodge in Ga. Eli A. Yoders opened their home as a makeshift clinic for interested persons desiring to be tested.

Dr. Rheims was on his way home after having visited in Lanc. and Delaware. Several from here will be going down for treatments. For those who are interested, but unaware of his techniques of testing, I understand he has a $1,000 a gallon liquid consisting of various chemicals that he uses on a patient's urine and sputum specimens that help him prophecy their present and future ailments.

perhaps the strongest preachers in favor of separation of church and state. Nor do they have life or any other kind of insurance for this would show they had no faith in God. Should an old couple, for reasons of ill health or disaster be left destitute, then relatives and the church will come to their aid. If they should have no children (as is sometimes the case) they may retire to the nearby small town. These town homes become a smaller version of their farms, with a small horse barn beside the house and much of the available land space turned into garden.

From "Portrait of Iowa"

When an Amishman retires it does not mean that he ceases to work, indeed he may work side-by-side with his sons and grandsons even up into his 90's. It only means that he has passed on the active decision making, but he always stands ready to advise the younger generation and his advice is usually heeded.

The old people spend their twilight years as loved and respected members of family and community. It is a time for them to enjoy what bounty the Lord has provided, to tell tales to grandchildren of memorable events in their own life or those of their forefathers.

From "Portrait of Iowa"

When finally they die even this is more softly, and with a greater sense of dignity. The Amish, as a whole, are very conscious of sickness and impending death and there is an acceptance of its place in life. If someone is ill he can expect all his family and friends to gather round. In the evening a steady stream of callers, friends, relatives and neighbors pay their respects to a family, perhaps staying no more than five minutes and saying but few words. News of a death spreads quickly and neighbors and non-relatives immediately take over the work load of the family.

THE BUDGET

FLEETWOOD, PA.

April 26—Burning wood is more popular since coal and oil prices are so high. In our Reading daily paper it is recommended people should burn as much wood as possible to warm their homes and as we drive along we see a lot of wood prepared to burn.

A wood fire gives sort of a pleasant smell, and might say its a little different in the woods. Beechwood fires are bright and clear, if the logs are kept a year. Chestnuts only good they say if its laid away a long time. Berch and Fur logs burn too fast, blaze up and do not last.

Elm wood burns like a church yard mold, even the very flames are cold.

Poplar gives a better smoke, fills your eyes and makes you choke.

Apple wood will scent your room with an incense like perfume. Oak and maple, if dry and old, will keep the winter cold, but ashwood wet and ashwood dry, just a little, a King can warm his feet.

THE BUDGET

DOVER, DELAWARE

Jan. 30—It is snowing since last night sometime but temperature is at 34, so not much snow on ground.

Wonder how many mothers or grandmothers know that when diaper pins stick, if you rub them on your hair or stick them in your hair bun, they will slide in diapers easily. I was 62 yrs. old before I learned that, but it really works.

The funeral will be a simple one with services in the home, then a procession of buggies to the graveside. The coffin is often made by Amish carpenters and had been made of walnut until the scarcity of this wood forced them to change to pine. In the strictest group the body may never leave the house until the day of the funeral and burial. Everything about the funeral and burial is plain, in keeping with their way of life and usually the expense is no more than $50.

All Amish cemeteries I have seen are particularly appropriate resting places for those whose whole life was farming. They all have been on high hills overlooking the farm that he or she had come to know and love—a place from which they might watch over the generations to come.

THE BUDGET

PINECRAFT, FLA.

July 29—Blessed with one-half inch of rainfall. Ground still dry and cracks in places of half inch wide. Hazy today and humid.

We got a couple hours fishing in too. Where they had chestnut trees and that was the first time he saw the chestnut burrs just in the starting stage since a boy at home. All these bring back fond memories of the good, old young days.

THE BUDGET

We wish to thank all neighbors and friends for everything during our sorrow.

We can only have one mother,
None else can take her place,
You can't tell how you'll need her,
Till you miss her loving face.

Quick and sudden was the call,
Mother's passing shocked us all,
A sudden change so quickly fell,
Without a chance to say farewell.

We mourn for you, dear companion,
But not with outward show,
For the heart that mourns sincerely,
Mourns silently and low.

From the grave we turned with sadness,
Turned away with heavy heart,
Turned away to face life's battles,
It was God's will! We part.

Looking back in memories,
Among life's road we trod,
We bless the years we had with you,
And leave the rest to God.

THE BUDGET

God needed another angel,
To fill His angel band,
So He came into our home one eve,
And took her by the hand.

Come now, Ruthie, come with me,
I need you in Heaven today,
My pretty mansions you shall see,
You'll be by my side to stay.

God loved you more, and thought it best,
To take you home to Heavenly rest,
Where we hope to meet you all some day,
Where no farewell tears will be shed.

Dear Ruthie has gone with the angels to
dwell,
Oh, how we miss you, no one can tell,
Ruthie has gone to meet brother Allan,
How happy two angels can be together in
Heaven.

Weep not for me, my parents and sisters
dear,
Since I must go and leave you here,
With Jesus, I shall happy be,
Oh, loved ones, do not weep for me.

Farewell, dear parents and sisters, too,
I leave you now to answer God's call,
Be faithful and true and prepare to meet
me,
Where there's a place prepared for us all.

THE BUDGET

Such a joyful experience we did share
When God placed that first born in our
care.
A picture of health and happiness was he,
And such a sweet smile for friends to see.

As you grew in body and mind, day by day,
Little did we think how soon you'd be
called away.
With your quiet manner, you'd run and
play,
Helping mommy and daddy in your
childish way.

From sixteen months on, you did not feel
well,
But where it hurt, you could not tell.
Many a time we'd rock you to sleep
Always striving these memories to keep.

We then learned, a tumor in your head
Caused the many restless hours in bed.
How often mommy and daddy walked the
floor,
Praying that for you, they could do more.

To ease the pain you so patiently bore,
Though often we mortals did wonder,
"what for?"
As we know you never did a wrong,
But He gave us strength to carry on.

To see an innocent suffer so,
Teaches a lesson, our Father does know,
How often we'd ask, "Can we stand the
test?"
Till our merciful God called our darling to
rest.

Oh, how often do the tears flow,
For dear Johnny, we miss you so!
Though we know you are free from all pain
evermore,
Let us all strive to meet on that bright
golden shore.

The lonely parents & brother

174